Early Learning

Reading Is All Around Us

Using Environmental Print to Teach Beginning Literacy Skills

Authors

Jennifer Prior, Ph.D. and Maureen R. Gerard, Ph.D.

SHELL EDUCATION

Editor
Jodene Smith, M.A.

Assistant Editor
Leslie Huber, M.A.

Editorial Director
Dona Herweck Rice

Editor-in-Chief
Sharon Coan, M.S.Ed.

Editorial Manager
Gisela Lee, M.A.

Creative Director
Lee Aucoin

Cover Design
Amy Couch

Illustration Manager/Designer
Timothy J. Bradley

Artists
Timothy J. Bradley
Daniel Jimenez

Print Production
Sandra Riley

Interior Layout Designer
Robin Erickson

Publisher

Corinne Burton, M.A.Ed

Standards Compendium, Copyright 2004 McREL

Shell Educational Publishing

5301 Oceanus Drive

Huntington Beach, California 92649

http://www.shelleducation.com

ISBN 978-1-4258-0049-9

© *2007 Shell Education*

Table of Contents

Introduction

The current thrust of education spending in the *No Child Left Behind Act* (U.S. Department of Education, 2000) is academic readiness. The sweeping legislation places greater emphasis on language acquisition and early reading development in preschool and the primary grades. Research supports the belief that reading success by third grade leads to later academic success (U.S. Department of Education, 2000).

Young children's early reading and writing proficiency is, therefore, an area of great interest both to policy makers and early-childhood professionals. "Early Reading First" guidelines (U.S. Department of Education, 2001) in *No Child Left Behind* include a program goal emphasizing the following:

- Oral language
- Phonological awareness
- Print awareness
- Alphabetic knowledge

A report from the National Institute of Child Health and Human Development widely known as the Report of the National Reading Panel (2000) has generated new research in early reading. Despite the reading research base drawn on by the National Reading panel, questions about young children's literacy development persist. How do children first begin to use written language? What can classroom teachers do to help all children to be successful in unlocking the alphabetic principle and the code system of written language? Early reading is an interwoven web of experiences, one part of which is children's early exposure to print in their world. Supplementing and enriching the curriculum with activities using familiar print provides an "auditory and visual anchor to remember letter symbol and sound" (Christie, et al, 2003a). By including activities with environmental print (the print found in a child's natural environment), teachers can provide opportunities for children to connect their prior knowledge to literacy experiences in school. Such experiences with familiar print assist children with word recognition and provide them with a sense of ownership when they recognize product logos and product labels that they see in their communities every day.

Organization of the Book

Chapter one, Learning to Read, focuses on the current research related to children's early reading abilities and the literacy knowledge they have upon entering school. Part of this literacy knowledge includes the awareness of environmental print. This chapter further develops how the National Reading Panel's five components of reading relate to children's early literacy knowledge and the bridge between purposeful uses of environmental print and the development of academic reading. Furthermore, the chapter will explain how to use this book to supplement any reading curriculum—preschool through first grade.

Introduction (cont.)

Chapter two, Phonological Awarness, examines phonological awareness as presented by the National Reading Panel's report. This includes a look at phonemic awareness, the alphabetic principle, and word building. Practical strategies for using environmental print to teach and reinforce skills in these areas are provided.

Chapter three, Fluency and Comprehension, focuses on fluency and comprehension skills. Environmental-print activities involving reading and rereading, meaning making, and writing are included.

The focus of chapter four, Building Vocabulary, is recognizing new words in print. Environmental-print activities in this chapter reinforce sight-word vocabulary, build vocabulary of high-frequency words, and engage children in the process of writing.

Chapters two, three, and four each provide lessons for direct, systematic instruction and individual practice with environmental print. In addition, each lesson offers ideas for differentiating instruction to meet the needs of a variety of learners.

Appenidixes B–E, provide ideas for adapting environmental-print lessons for a variety of learners, including English-language learners and advanced learners. These ideas can easily be applied to the lessons provided within this book.

This book will guide the early childhood educator and the pre-service teacher with a variety of ideas for enriching an existing comprehensive integrated curriculum for young children with environmental-print connections. You will find that encounters with environmental-print activities assist children in making connections between literacy experiences at home and those at school.

Standards Correlation

Shell Educational Publishing is committed to producing educational materials that are research- and standards-based. In this effort, we have correlated all of our products to the academic standards of all 50 states, the District of Columbia, and the Department of Defense Dependent Schools. You can print a correlation report customized for your state directly from our website at **http://www.shelleducation.com**.

Purpose and Intent of Standards

The No Child Left Behind legislation mandates that all states adopt academic standards that identify the skills students will learn in kindergarten through grade twelve. While many states had already adopted academic standards prior to NCLB, the legislation set requirements to ensure the standards were detailed and comprehensive.

Standards are designed to focus instruction and guide adoption of curricula. Standards are statements that describe the criteria necessary for students to meet specific academic goals. They define the knowledge, skills, and content students should acquire at each level. Standards are also used to develop standardized tests to evaluate students' academic progress.

In many states today, teachers are required to demonstrate how their lessons meet state standards. State standards are used in development of all of our products, so educators can be assured they meet the academic requirements of each state. Complete standards correlation reports for each state can be printed directly from our website as well.

How to Find Standards Correlations

To print a correlation report for this product, visit our website at **http://www.shelleducation.com** and follow the on-screen directions. If you require assistance in printing correlation reports, contact Customer Service at 1-877-777-3450.

Standards Correlation Chart

Standard	Benchmark	Lesson and Page Number
Standard 1 Uses the general skills and strategies of the writing process	1.6 (Level: K–2) Uses writing and other methods (e.g., using letters or phonetically spelled words, telling, dictating, making lists) to describe familiar persons, places, objects, or experiences	Environmental-Print ABC Big Book 71–72 Writing with Environmental Print 82–83 Writing a Personal "My Letter Book" with Environmental Print 84–86 Pattern Book with Environmental Print 87–102 Rebus Writing with Environmental Print 107–108
Standard 5 Uses the general skills and strategies of the reading process	5.3 (Level: K–2) Uses basic elements of phonetic analysis (e.g., common letter/sound relationships, beginning and ending consonants, vowel sounds, blends, word patterns) to decode unknown words	Beginning Sound Matching 14–15 Ending Sound Identification 16–17 Silly Sound Substitution 18–19 Categorization and Beginning-Sound Isolation 20–24 Ending-Sound Isolation 25–26 Alliteration Songs 32–33 Isolating Sounds 34–39 Letter Posters 40–41 Letter Hunt 42–45 Beginning-Letter Match 46–47 Puzzle Spelling 48–51 Decontextualized Reading 52–53 Sounding out Words 54–56 Identifying Blends 57–58 Long Vowels or Short Vowels 59–60 CVC Words 61–62 R-Controlled Vowels 63–65 Environmental-Print ABC Big Book 71–72 Environmental-Print ABC Little Book 73–81 Writing a Personal "My Letter Book" with Environmental Print 84–86
	5.4 (Level: K–2) Uses basic elements of structural analysis (e.g., syllables, basic prefixes, suffixes, root words, compound words, spelling patterns, contractions) to decode unknown words	Rhyming 27–28 Counting Syllables 29–31

Standards Correlation Chart (cont.)

Standard	Benchmark	Lesson and Page Number
Standard 5 (*cont.*) Uses the general skills and strategies of the reading process	5.6 (Level: K–2) Understands level-appropriate sight words and vocabulary (e.g., words for persons, places, things, actions; high-frequency words such as said, was, and where)	Environmental-Print Word Wall 67–68 Word Wall Reading Sponge Activities 69–70 Pattern Book with Environmental Print 87–102 Rebus Reading in a Morning Message 103–104 Rebus Language Experience with Environmental Print 105–106 "Go Fish" Reading 115–116 Environmental-Print Word Sort 134–135 Environmental-Print Word Sort with a Venn Diagram 136–138 Word Mapping with Environmental Print 139–141 Mapping Experiences with Environmental-Print Words 142–144 My Very Own Word Bank 145–147 Teaching Simple Analogies with Environmental Print 148–149 Word Sorting with Body Percussion 150 – 151 Compound Words in Environmental Print 152–153 Sketch to Stretch for Compound Words 154–155 Decontextualized Vocabulary Collage 156–157 Vocabulary Bingo 158–160 Find the Common Word 161–162 If You Can Read This… 163–165 Can You Read it Now? 166–169
	5.8 (Level: K–2) Reads aloud familiar stories, poems, and passages with fluency and expression (e.g., rhythm, flow, meter, tempo, pitch, tone, intonation)	Environmental-Print Word Wall 67–68 Pattern Book with Environmental Print 87–102 Rebus Reading in a Morning Message 103–104 Rebus Language Experience with Environmental Print 105–106 Echo Reading 109–110 Paired Reading 111–112 Spin the Bottle Reading 113–114
	5.9 (Level: Pre-K) Knows familiar print in their environment (e.g., traffic signs, store logos)	All lessons
Standard 7 Uses reading skills and strategies to understand and interpret a variety of informational texts.	7.1 (Level: K–2) Uses reading skills and strategies to understand a variety of informational texts (e.g., written directions, signs, captions, warning labels, informational books)	Class Survey Book 117—122 Environmental-Print ABC Big Book 71–72 Writing with Environmental Print 82–83 Writing a Personal "My Letter Book" with Environmental Print 84–86 Pattern Book with Environmental Print 87–102 Rebus Writing with Environmental Print 107–108 Stories in a Bag 123–124 Circular Storytelling with Environmental Print 125–126 What's Going On Here? Critical Literacy with Environmental Print 127–128 3-D Environmental-Print Counting Book 129–130 What's Going On Here? Critical Literacy with Environmental Print #2 131–132

Learning to Read

Early childhood teachers have much to consider as they negotiate instructional strategies in their own classroom settings. Decades of research (Berry, 2001; Christie, Enz, and Vukelich, 2002; Ferreiro and Teberosky, 1982; Goodman, 1986; Harste, Burke, and Woodward, 1982) suggest that children start developing early literacy skills through their day-to-day experiences in a print-rich literate society. Children's prior knowledge of print in the environment—signs, billboards, logos, and functional print that saturate a child's world—can be used by teachers to make a meaningful bridge between what children already know and what they encounter in the school curriculum (Christie, Enz, Gerard, and Prior, 2003a; Christie, et al, 2003a; Duke and Purcell-Gates, 2003; Orellana and Hernadez, 2003; Xu and Rutledge, 2003). Purposeful planned encounters with environmental print can assist children in making connections between print in the home, print in the community, and school literacy experiences.

Teachers can assist young children to become proficient readers and writers in many ways. The National Association for the Education of Young Children (2001) suggests the integrated use of speaking, listening, reading, and writing in the following ways:

- Provide social experiences for using language purposefully.
- Use reading and speaking to support oral language and vocabulary development.
- Use the home language and culture to introduce new words and concepts.
- Build on children's experiences.
- Provide opportunities to write.
- Play with language to develop phonemic awareness.
- Build knowledge of letters, sounds, and words.

Simmons, Gunn, Smith, and Kameenui (1994) stress the importance of teaching letters and sounds for reading success. They suggest the teaching of phonemic awareness through segmenting and blending sounds. While the awareness of sound units in phonemes, syllables, and words is a strong indicator of later reading success, keep in mind that, above all, reading is a meaning-making process. Letter and sound correspondences are beginning components of learning to read, but the comprehension of text is why children learn to read.

Satisfaction and enjoyment, the power of human interaction, the communication of important messages, pleasure and delight in the words themselves along with the ability to match letters to sounds overlay the skills of decoding. Phonemic awareness, the knowledge of rhyming, blending, and segmenting of letter sounds, serves as knowledge only if embedded in meaningful experiences. It is our responsibility as educators to provide meaningful experiences for our students.

What Is Environmental Print?

Environmental print is defined as product and restaurant logos, signs, billboards, advertising, and functional print (street signs, door signs, etc.) commonly found in a child's environment. This is not to be confused with "print in the environment" which can encompass a variety of forms, such as teacher labeling of objects in the environment.

Environmental print first appeared on the education forefront when researchers found that very young children were able to read print in their surroundings. In a study by Harste, Burke, and Woodward (1982), it was determined that three- to six-year-old children could read environmental print. Anderson and Markle (1985) suggested discussing environmental print items to create meaningful experiences for children. Cloer, Aldridge and Dean (1981,1982), encouraged teachers to use environmental print to assist children in the transition from reading environmental print to reading manuscript through instruction.

There has been some question, however, as to whether or not children attend to the individual sounds and symbols of environmental print. In fact, the studies with environmental print lay dormant during the 1990s after Masonheimer, Drum, and Ehri (1984) debunked environmental print reading as not reading at all. They reported that the absence of visual and contextual cues prevented children from recognizing the words.

Renewed interest in the role of environmental print came about in the early 2000s when numerous studies (Christie, et al, 2002; Prior and Gerard, 2004) found that adult interaction with children was key to the transfer to conventional reading. The researchers report that the adult must draw attention to the letters and sounds in environmental-print words in order for children to recognize environmental print as words rather than pictures.

Why the Five Components of Reading?

The Report from the National Reading Panel (National Institute of Child Health and Human Development, 2000) marked a qualitative shift in beginning reading and writing instruction across the United States. It has generated new early reading standards, new curriculum approaches, and new classroom practices. The *No Child Left Behind* legislation has taken the outcomes of the National Reading Panel report and translated these into very specific "Reading First" guidelines. These guidelines specify that instructional programs be based in valid scientific research and address the learning needs of all students, including high and low achievers, second-language learners, and special education students. The guidelines further specify five essential components in high quality reading instruction that emerged from the report of the National Reading Panel: 1.) Phonemic Awareness, 2.) Phonics, 3.) Fluency, 4.) Comprehension, 5.) Vocabulary. While many other components of reading instruction are very important to the multidimensional task of learning to read, the NRP report focuses on these five components.

Phonemic awareness instruction should provide explicit instruction that focuses in letter-sound relationships, segmenting, and blending. The "Reading First" guidelines look for early linkage between sounds and letter symbols, even before letter names are learned, as well as ongoing assessment of phonemic awareness skills to inform instruction.

Phonics and word study instruction, according to the National Reading Panel, should also be explicit, systematic instruction that teaches letter-sound connections and blending skills to read whole words. These same skills must be applied to learning to spell. Reading text demands that students immediately apply their phonics knowledge to decode and comprehend what is being read. And, as with phonemic awareness instruction, phonics and word study skills must be systematically assessed to inform continued instruction.

Fluency instruction appears in the NRP report as an essential component of reading. The "Reading First" guidelines call for opportunities for oral repeated reading that are supported by the teacher, by peers, and at home by family members. The text that students read and reread should be well matched to their reading skills and should build rate and accuracy of oral reading.

Comprehension instruction, not surprisingly, appears in the Report of the National Reading Panel as an essential component of reading instruction. This must include teaching before, during, and after reading both narrative and informational text. Teachers must explicitly explain and model strategies that aid comprehension. Discussion techniques and questioning strategies must also be directly explained and modeled by the teacher. Extended opportunities must be provided to struggling readers—low readers, ELL students, and special-needs students—to participate and be included in successful reading.

Vocabulary instruction is the fifth component of the National Reading Panel report. Vocabulary instruction, according to "Reading First" guidelines, must also be direct, systematic, and explicit. The meanings of words and word-learning strategies must be taught by the teacher. Structural analysis of words and the etymology of words must be taught as well.

The lessons in this book are arranged to meet the five components of reading instruction as outlined in the Report of the National Reading Panel. The research evidence base for including environmental print in early reading instruction supports the goals of "Reading First" and instruction in the five component areas.

Supplementing the Reading Curriculum

The key to using environmental print, as research indicates (Christie, et al, 2002 and 2003b and Prior and Gerard, 2004), is interaction with an adult. Children typically see environmental print and logos as meaningful pictures, but when the adult draws attention to the letters in familiar print, children begin to make the transition to conventional reading skills.

A curriculum of environmental print supplements the standard curriculum by providing additional whole- and small-group lessons along with independent and small-group practice in learning centers. Keep in mind that the selected print items should be those that are familiar to the children. Since children will readily recognize the environmental print and print items you choose, these activities can be implemented from the beginning of the school year and will actually bring a level of comfort and familiarity to the students as they bridge beginning reading with their everyday environment.

Phonological Awareness

There are countless ways to use environmental print to teach phonological awareness skills. Interaction with print that is familiar to students creates an excellent cognitive anchor for teaching the sounds and symbols of written language.

Phonemic Awareness

Phonemic awareness refers to a person's ability to attend to and manipulate the sounds of spoken words. In order to begin reading, a child needs to understand that words are made up of individual sounds. Phonemic awareness activities are playful and fun and greatly enhanced when combined with environmental print. As described in the report of The National Reading Panel, there are several elements involved in phonemic awareness instruction. These include phoneme isolation, phoneme identity, phoneme categorization, phoneme blending, phoneme segmentation, phoneme deletion, phoneme addition, and phoneme substitution. This section provides lessons and activities for using environmental print to draw attention to the sounds that make up words.

The Alphabetic Principle

Phonemic awareness assists children in spelling and should be related to letters in order to assist them with transitioning from hearing sounds to reading words. Phonics skills help children learn the relationships between the letters of written language and the sounds of spoken language. This leads to an understanding of the alphabetic principle.

In order for phonics instruction to be most effective, it should be introduced early in the child's school experience. Phonics is a necessary part of a well-balanced program.

In this section, you'll find a variety of environmental-print lessons. These lessons and activities will assist you with creative ideas for teaching phonemic awareness skills and the alphabetic principle by incorporating environmental print.

Beginning–Sound Matching

Activity Format

Whole group

Objective

Students will identify beginning letter sounds and sort words by beginning letter sounds.

Materials

- a supply of environmental-print words (six beginning with **b**, six beginning with **m**, and six beginning with **d**)
- three library pockets
- poster board
- glue
- scissors

Preparation

1. Glue three library pockets to a piece of poster board.
2. Glue a different environmental-print word to the front of each pocket, one beginning with **b**, one beginning with **m**, and one beginning with **d** (for example, *Barney*™, *McDonald's*™, and *Disney*™).
3. Prepare a set of environmental-print words—five beginning with **b**, five beginning with **m**, and five beginning with **d**. Environmental-print words can be cut from newspaper ads, product packaging, and coupons, or printed from the computer.
4. Laminate the environmental-print words for durability, if desired.

Procedure

1. Gather the students together. Show the students the pocket board. Ask the students to identify the words on the pocket board. Draw the students' attention to the letter sound heard at the beginning of each word. For example, if one word is *Burger King*™, emphasize the /b/ sound.

2. Review the other words with the students. One-by-one, ask them to identify each word.

3. Then, say a word slowly from the prepared set of environmental-print words, emphasizing the beginning letter sound.

4. Ask the students to identify which word on the pocket board has the same beginning sound. (At this point, emphasize the sounds rather than the letters.)

5. When matching beginning sounds are identified, place the word in the corresponding pocket.

6. Continue in this manner with the remaining environmental-print words.

Beginning–Sound Matching (cont.)

Sample Dialog

Teacher:	What is this word?
Student:	*Band-Aid*™
Teacher:	Let's listen to the sound at the beginning of *Band-Aid*. (Emphasize the /b/ sound.) What sound do you hear? (Encourage the students to identify the sound rather than the letter.)
Student:	/b/
Teacher:	Yes, *Band-Aid* begins with the /b/ sound. Which word on the pockets also begins with the /b/ sound?
Student:	*Barney*!
Teacher:	That's right! *Barney* and *Band-Aid* both begin with the /b/ sound. Let's place *Band-Aid* in the *Barney* pocket. Let's look at another word.

Assessment

Observe the students' participation during the activity. Pay attention to students' abilities to identify the sounds at the beginnings of the words. If necessary, take extra time to emphasize the beginning sounds.

Differentiation

- Place the materials at a learning center and encourage the students to sort words independently.
- Conduct the same activity with a small group of students. Provide assistance to the students who struggle with the identification of letter sounds.

Ending-Sound Identification

Activity Format

Whole group

Objective

Students will identify ending letter sounds and sort words by ending letter sounds.

Materials

- a supply of environmental-print words (including some that end with **s**)
- sheet of construction paper
- marker
- scissors
- tape (or other temporary adhesive)

Preparation

1. Use the marker to write the letter **s** on the sheet of construction paper.
2. Prepare a set of environmental-print words—several should end with the letter **s** (*Froot Loops*™, *Corn Pops*™, *Corn Flakes*™, *Skittles*™, *Life Savers*™, *Lay's*™). The environmental-print words can be cut from newspaper ads, product packaging, and coupons, or printed from the computer.
3. Laminate the environmental-print words for durability, if desired.

Procedure

1. Gather the students together. Display the construction paper labeled with the letter **s**. Ask the students to identify the sound of the letter **s.** Then, ask the students to think of words they know that begin with the /s/ sound.
2. Next, say the word *glass*. Emphasize the /s/ sound at the end of the word. Ask the children to pay close attention to the sound they hear at the end of the word.
3. Challenge the children to think of words that end in /s/.
4. Tell the students that they will be asked to read a set of words. Their job is to identify the words that end with /s/.
5. One at a time, hold up an environmental-print word. Ask the students to say the word. Then, repeat the word, emphasizing the ending sound. If the word ends with /s/, tape it near the **s** on the construction paper. If the word does not end with /s/, set it to the side.
6. Continue in this manner with the remaining environmental-print words.

Ending–Sound Identification (cont.)

Sample Dialog

Teacher: What is this word?

Student: *Corn Flakes*

Teacher: I'm going to say the word again. Listen to the sound you hear at the end of *Corn Flakes*. (Emphasize the /s/ sound.) What sound do you hear? (Encourage the students to identify the sound rather than the letter.)

Student: /s/

Teacher: Yes, the /s/ sound is heard at the end of *Corn Flakes*.

Assessment

Observe the students' participation during the activity. Pay attention to students' abilities to identify the sounds at the ends of the words. If necessary, take extra time to emphasize the ending sounds.

Differentiation

- Place the materials at a learning center and encourage the students to repeat the activity independently.
- Conduct the same activity with a small group of students. Provide assistance to the students who struggle with the identification of letter sounds.
- Challenge the students to repeat the activity identifying words with different ending sounds.

Silly Sound Substitution

Activity Format

Whole group

Objective

Students will substitute beginning letter sounds to create silly words.

Materials

- a supply of environmental-print words
- scissors

Preparation

1. Prepare a set of familiar environmental-print words to use for the activity. Environmental print can be cut from newspaper ads, product packaging, and coupons, or printed from the computer. Keep in mind that environmental print also consists of functional print, such as the name of your school, a stop sign, or an exit sign.

2. Laminate the environmental-print words for durability, if desired.

Procedure

1. Gather the students together. Hold up an environmental-print word, such as *McDonald's*.

2. Ask the students to listen carefully to the beginning sound they hear in the word. Assist them, if necessary, with identifying the sound.

3. Tell the students that they will play a silly game where they will change the beginning sound of words.

4. Ask the students how the word *McDonald's* would change if the /m/ were changed to /r/. Lead the students to say *RcDonald's*.

5. One at a time, hold up an environmental-print word. Ask the students to say the word. Have them identify the beginning sound. Then, give them a different sound to substitute for the beginning sound. Have the students say the new silly word.

6. Continue in this manner with the remaining environmental-print words.

Silly Sound Substitution (cont.)

Sample Dialog

Teacher: What is this word?

Student: *Sesame Street*™

Teacher: I'm going to say the word again. Listen to the sound you hear at the beginning of the words. (Emphasize the /s/ sound.) What sound do you hear? (Encourage the students to identify the sound rather than the letter.)

Student: /s/

Teacher: That's right. *Sesame* and *Street* each begin with /s/. Now, say *Sesame Street* again.

Student: *Sesame Street*

Teacher: How would *Sesame Street* sound if we changed the /s/ to /w/?

Student: *Wesame Weet*

Teacher: Good! When we change the /s/ to /w/, we get silly words—*Wesame* and *Weet*.

Assessment

Observe the students' participation during the activity. Pay attention to students' abilities to substitute the sounds at the beginnings of words. If necessary, take extra time to emphasize the sounds.

Differentiation

- Place the materials at a learning center and encourage the students to repeat the activity independently.
- Conduct the same activity with a small group of students. Provide assistance to the students who struggle with the identification of letter sounds.

Phonological Awareness

Categorization and Beginning– Sound Isolation

Activity Format

Whole group

Objective

Students will identify beginning letter sounds of words and place them in categories.

Materials

- "Category Cards" (pages 22–24)
- a supply of environmental-print words
- tape or putty-like adhesive
- scissors

Preparation

1. Duplicate the category cards on cardstock paper. Cut out the cards.
2. Prepare a set of familiar environmental-print words to use for the activity. For this activity, be sure to use words that match the category labels you select. For example, if you choose to use the labels "Places We Eat" and "Things We Play With," select environmental-print words that fall in these categories. Environmental print can be cut from newspaper ads, product packaging, and coupons, or printed from the computer.
3. Laminate the environmental-print words and category labels for durability, if desired.

Procedure

1. Select two category labels, such as "Places We Eat" and "Things We Play With." Affix these labels to the wall or board.
2. Gather the students together. Review the category names and invite the students to discuss the things that come to mind when they think of these.
3. Tell the students that they are going to read words and decide whether they are names of places where we eat or whether they are names of toys or playthings.
4. Display an environmental-print word, such as LEGO™. Ask the students to identify the word. Ask the students whether LEGO is a place to eat or something to play with.
5. Adhere the word to the wall below the label "Things We Play With."
6. Continue in this manner with the remaining environmental-print words.
7. When all of the words have been categorized, take time to review them.
8. Ask the students to identify the beginning letter sound heard in each one.
9. Then, group words with the same beginning sounds.

Categorization and Beginning–Sound Isolation (cont.)

Sample Dialog

Teacher:	What is this word?
Student:	LEGO
Teacher:	Right. These letters spell the word LEGO. What is LEGO? Is it a place where we eat or something we play with?
Student:	It's something we play with.
Teacher:	Have you ever played with LEGOs before?
Student:	Yes, I have LEGOs at my house.
Teacher:	In which category should we place this word?
Student:	Things We Play With
Teacher:	You are right! LEGOs are toys we play with. Now, let's look at the words in the two categories. Let's determine the sound at the beginning of each word.

Assessment

Observe the students' participation during the activity. Allow each student the opportunity to identify letter sounds by saying them aloud to the group or to a partner. Make note of students who struggle with beginning-sound isolation or categorizing.

Differentiation

- At a learning center, post category labels on the wall or simply set them on a table. Encourage the children to sort words independently or in small groups.
- Conduct the same activity with a small group of students. Provide assistance to the students who struggle with the identification of letter sounds.
- For the students who need an added challenge, ask them to group the environmental-print words by the same ending sound.
- For an additional challenge, ask the students to write a list of words they know that would fall into the selected categories.

Category Cards

Places We Eat

Things We Play With

Category Cards (cont.)

Favorite Toys

Favorite Snacks

Category Cards (cont.)

Places We Shop

Things We Drink

Ending–Sound Isolation

Activity Format

Whole group

Objective

Students will identify ending letter sounds of words.

Materials

- a supply of environmental-print words
- index cards
- scissors
- glue

Preparation

1. On each of several index cards, glue two environmental-print words that have the same ending sound, such as Jell-O™ and LEGO. (Select words with several different ending sounds.)

2. Laminate the cards for durability, if desired.

Procedure

1. Tell the students that they will pay attention to the ending sounds of words in this activity.

2. Say a word aloud, such as *bat*. Ask the students to identify the sound they hear at the end of the word *bat*. Emphasize the /t/ sound, if necessary.

3. Have the students use the word *bat* in the following chant:

   bat, bat, bat /t//t//t/

   bat, bat, bat /t//t//t/

4. Have them try chanting words with different ending sounds.

5. Next, ask a student volunteer to select a word card. Ask the student to say aloud the two words on the card.

6. Ask the students to identify the sound that is the same at the end of each word.

7. Repeat the words as needed to assist the students with identifying the ending sounds they hear.

8. Continue in this manner with the remainder of the cards.

Ending–Sound Isolation (cont.)

Sample Dialog

Teacher: (Teacher asks a student to select a card.) Read the words on the card.

Student: LEGO and *Jell-O*.

Teacher: LEGO and *Jell-O*. (Emphasize the /o/ sound.) What sound do you hear at the end of both of these words?

Student: /o/

Teacher: That's right. *Jell-O* ends with /o/ and LEGO ends with /o/. Can you think of other words that end with /o/?

Student: *Snow*

Teacher: Yes! *Jell*-O, LEGO, and *snow* all have /o/ at the end. Now, let's identify ending sounds on the other cards.

Assessment

Observe each student's ability to identify the ending sounds. Make note of students who struggle with ending letter identification.

Differentiation

- Place the cards at a learning center and have the students repeat this activity independently.
- Conduct the same activity with a small group of students. Provide assistance to the students who struggle with the identification of letter sounds.
- Create a set of cards with matching beginning letter sounds. Have the students use these cards in the same manner as the lesson.
- Mix up the beginning letter and ending letter cards for more of a challenge. The students must determine whether the words on the cards have the same beginning sound or the same ending sound.

Rhyming

<table>
<tr><td>

Activity Format

Whole group

Objective

Students will identify environmental-print words that rhyme.

Materials

- a supply of environmental-print words (each word should rhyme with at least one other word)
- chalkboard or whiteboard
- chalk or markers
- scissors
- index cards
- glue

</td><td>

Preparation

1. Cut out several environmental-print words. Each word should rhyme with another word. Here are some examples:

   Eggo™/LEGO   Kix™/Trix™/Twix™

   Barbie™/Arby('s)™   stop/Corn Pop(s)

   Rugrat™/Kit Kat™   Frito™/Dorito™

2. Glue each environmental-print word to an index card.

3. Laminate the label cards for durability, if desired.

Procedure

1. Gather the students together. Say the words *Jelly Belly*™ aloud.

2. Ask the students what they notice about the words. If necessary, slowly say the words again drawing the students' attention to the sounds of the words.

3. The children will likely notice that the words sound the same in some way.

4. Have the children say the words *Jelly Belly* along with you. Then, ask them to think of other words that sound the same.

5. Point out each time the two words begin with different letters, but the remainder of the words sound the same. Explain that these are called rhyming words.

6. Display a word, such as *Kix*. Tell students that their job will be to find another word that rhymes with *Kix*.

7. Next, hold up another word that doesn't rhyme and say both words. Ask the students if the two words sound the same.

8. Then, hold up the two words that rhyme, such as *Trix* and *Kix*. Ask the students if the words sound the same.

</td></tr>
</table>

Rhyming (cont.)

Sample Dialog

Teacher:	(Teacher holds up the K*ix* label.) What does this word say?
Student:	K*ix*
Teacher:	Let's try to find another word that rhymes with K*ix*. (Teacher holds up J*ell*-O.) What does this word say?
Student:	J*ell*-O
Teacher:	Let's say these two words together.
Student:	K*ix*, J*ell*-O
Teacher:	Do K*ix* and J*ell*-O sound alike?
Student:	No!
Teacher:	(Holds up the T*rix* label card.) Let's say this word together.
Student:	T*rix*
Teacher:	K*ix* and T*rix*. Do these words sound alike?
Student:	Yes!

Assessment

Observe the students' abilities to read the words. Pay attention to the students' abilities to identify rhyming words.

Differentiation

- Place the label cards at a learning center and have the students repeat this activity independently.
- For a challenge, ask the students to write lists of words (real or nonsense) that rhyme.

Counting Syllables

Activity Format

Whole group

Objective

Students will identify the number of syllables in words.

Materials

- a supply of environmental-print words
- pliable adhesive or tape
- scissors
- "Syllables Chart" (page 31)

Preparation

1. Prepare a set of familiar environmental-print words to use for the activity.

2. Environmental print can be cut from newspaper ads, product packaging, and coupons, or printed from the computer. Keep in mind that environmental print also consists of functional print, such as the name of your school, a stop sign, or an exit sign.

3. Laminate the environmental-print words for durability, if desired.

4. Photocopy the "Syllables Chart."

Procedure

1. Gather the students together. Hold up one of the environmental-print words, such as Cheerios™.

2. Ask the students to listen carefully to the word as you say it again. Clap your hands for each syllable as you say it.

3. Affix the word to the board for students to see. Ask the students to clap the number of "beats" or syllables in the word. Then, point out that Cheerios has three beats (or syllables).

4. Try this activity again with a word with a different number of syllables, such as LEGO.

5. Affix the word to the board. Ask the students to clap the beats as they say the word—LE-GO. Point to the parts of the words as the children clap.

6. Ask the students how many beats they hear in LEGO.

7. Continue in this manner with the remaining words.

8. For additional practice, distribute copies of the "Syllables Chart" and have each student glue an environmental-print word in the first space. Then, have the student cut another copy of the same word to divide it into syllables. The student glues the pieces to the chart and then writes the number of syllables.

Counting Syllables (cont.)

Sample Dialog

Teacher: (Holds up the word *Cheerios*.) What does this word say?

Student: *Cheerios*!

Teacher: I'm going to say the word again and clap at the same time. Listen carefully as I say the word. *Cheer-i-os*. (Teacher claps each syllable.) How many times did I clap? Let's try it again. *Cheer-i-os*.

Student: Three

Teacher: That's right. I clapped three times. *Cheer-i-os* has three beats. Let's try another one. (Teacher holds up the word *Barbie*.) Let's clap as we say *Barbie*.

Student: *Bar-bie*

Teacher: How many times did we clap?

Student: Two times.

Teacher: Great! You figured out that *Bar-bie* has two beats. We can also call "beats" syllables. Let's try another word.

Assessment

Observe the students' active participation during the activity. Each student should clap the syllables in each featured word. Assist students who struggle with this.

Differentiation

- Challenge the students by having them identify syllables in longer words or in product names that have more than one word, such as *Tootsie Roll*™, *Teletubbies*™, *Domino's Pizza*™, etc.
- Conduct the same activity with a small group of students. Have the students practice identifying syllables in environmental-print words and in other words.
- The students who struggle with this skill may need to use more physical movement. Have these students pat their chests as they say the words or stand and stomp on the floor.

Syllables Chart

Word	Syllables	Total

Alliteration Songs

Activity Format

Whole group

Objective

Students will identify a series of words beginning with the same sound.

Materials

- a supply of environmental-print words
- chalkboard or whiteboard
- scissors
- tape or pliable adhesive

Preparation

1. Prepare sets of logos or environmental-print words that begin with the same sound.
2. Logos and environmental print can be cut from newspaper ads, product packaging, and coupons, or printed from the computer. Keep in mind that environmental print also consists of functional print, such as the name of your school, a stop sign, or an exit sign.
3. Laminate the logos and environmental-print words for durability, if desired.

Procedure

1. Gather the students together and post the environmental-print words beginning with the same sound on the board.
2. Create a song using the words. For example, the following song can be sung to the tune of "Mary Had a Little Lamb."

   Sesame Street and Skittles, Skittles, Skittles
   Sesame Street and Skittles make me want to STOP.

3. After singing the song once, invite the students to sing it again along with you. Point to the words on the board as you sing.
4. Ask the students to listen for the sound heard at the beginning of many of the words. If necessary, sing the song again, emphasizing the /s/ sound.
5. Continue in this manner with other alliterative songs. Use the songs on the next page, if desired.

Alliteration Songs (cont.)

Sample Songs

Sing to the tune of "London Bridge Is Falling Down."

Barbie, Barney, Blue's Clues™, Blue's Clues, Blue's Clues

Barbie, Barney, Blue's Clues

Burger King and Band-Aid

Sing to the tune of "The Itsy Bitsy Spider."

Pizza Hut™ and Play-Doh™

PEPSI™ and Pokemon™

Pizza Hut and Play-Doh

PEPSI Pokemon

Sing to the tune of "Alouette"

Teletubbie, Total™, and Taco Bell™

Tootsie Roll and Toys "R" Us™

Assessment

Observe the students' participation as they sing the song. Be sure that all students understand that each song has many words beginning with the same sound.

Differentiation

- Record the songs and allow the students time at a listening center to listen and sing.
- Encourage the students to create their own alliterative songs. Allow them to perform their songs for the class.
- Help struggling students by emphasizing the beginning sounds of words. For example, say with the child, "*Band-Aid /b//b//b/—Band-Aid /b//b//b/.*"

Isolating Sounds

Activity Format

Small group/
Independent practice

Objective

Students will identify sounds in words.

Materials

- "Functional-Print Cards" (pages 36–39)
- a supply of environmental-print words
- scissors
- glue
- index cards

Preparation

1. Duplicate and cut out "Functional-Print Cards."
2. Glue each environmental-print word and functional print word to an index card.
3. Laminate the cards for durability, if desired.

Procedure

1. Gather a small group of students. (This activity will first be done in a small group and then independently by the students.)
2. Show the students the cards and explain that they will identify the first sound they hear in each word.
3. Ask a child to select a card from the stack and have him or her say the word and then tell the beginning letter sound. (Be sure to focus on the beginning sound rather than the name of the letter.)
4. Challenge the children to think of other words that begin with the same sound.
5. Then, ask the child to identify the sound heard at the end of the word.
6. Continue in this manner, giving all the students in the group the chance to select a card and identify the sound. (Depending on the number of cards prepared for the activity, each child in the group should have several turns.)
7. After having the children participate in this activity in a small group, encourage them to play independently for further practice.

Isolating Sounds (cont.)

Sample Dialog

Teacher: What word is on the card?

Student: *Stop*

Teacher: What sound do you hear at the beginning of the word *Stop*?

Student: /s/

Teacher: Right. What sound do you hear at the end of the word *Stop*?

Student: /p/

Teacher: Can you think of another word that begins with /s/?

Student: (Students respond.)

Assessment

Observe each student's ability to identify the beginning and ending sounds of the words. Pay attention to the student's ability to think of other words that begin with the same sound.

Differentiation

- For an added challenge, ask the students to identify the consonant sounds in the middle of words.
- Place the cards at a learning center. Have the students match cards that have the same beginning or ending sounds.

Functional-Print Cards

Girls

Boys

Functional-Print Cards (cont.)

Functional–Print Cards (cont.)

Functional–Print Cards (cont.)

Letter Posters

Activity Format

Small group

Objective

Students will locate words beginning with featured letters.

Materials

- a supply of environmental-print words
- chalkboard or whiteboard
- chalk or marker
- crayons
- sheets of construction paper
- scissors
- glue

Preparation

1. Determine a letter to feature in this lesson, such as **T**.
2. Cut out several environmental-print words that are familiar to the students. Several of the words should begin with the featured letter, along with others that do not. There should be at least four words beginning with the featured sound for each child.

Procedure

1. Gather a small group of students.
2. Write the letter pair **T/t** (or another selected letter pair) on the board. Ask the students to identify the letter and the sound it represents.
3. Tell the students that they will each make a collage of words that begin with the letter **T**.
4. Distribute a large sheet of construction paper to each child.
5. Instruct each child to use a crayon to write the featured letter in the center of the sheet of construction paper.
6. Next, spread out the collection of environmental-print words for all students in the group to see. Tell the students that they should look for words that begin with the letter **T**.
7. When a child finds a **T** word, have him or her glue it to the construction paper, making sure not to cover the letter written in the center.
8. The child continues in this manner until he or she has glued four words beginning with that letter.
9. Ask each student to read the words on his or her collage and identify the sound at the beginning of each word.

Letter Posters (cont.)

Sample Dialog

Teacher: Write the letter **T** in the center of your paper. What sound does the letter **T** make?

Student: /t/

Teacher: Can you think of some words that begin with the /t/ sound?

Student: *Tire* (Allow several students to share.)

Teacher: Look at the words on this table. Some of the words begin with **T** and others do not. Does *Subway*™ begin with **T**?

Student: No! It begins with **S**.

Teacher: What about *Taco Bell*? Does *Taco* begin with **T**?

Student: Yes!

Teacher: Great! Now your job is to find four words that begin with **T** and glue them to your paper.

Assessment

Review each child's collage, looking for at least four environmental-print words beginning with the featured letter. Listen as the child reads the words he or she selected and repeats the sound heard at the beginning of each word.

Differentiation

- For an added challenge, select two featured letters. Have each child fold the paper in half and label each side with a different letter. The child glues words corresponding with the featured letters on the paper.
- For the students who need additional practice with letter sounds rather than letter identification, focus on the sound at the beginning of each environmental-print word. Emphasize the sound rather than the letter itself.

Letter Hunt

Activity Format

Small group

Objective

Students will identify the beginning letters of words and find these letters on a chart.

Materials

- "Letter Chart" (pages 44 and 45)
- a supply of environmental-print words (only one word for each letter—all letters of the alphabet do not need to be represented)
- scissors
- glue
- squares of paper or plastic game markers

Preparation

1. Duplicate "Letter Chart" for each child in the small group.
2. Glue the two pages of the letter chart together on the glue tab. Laminate each chart for durability, if desired.
3. Cut out a supply of environmental-print words. Be sure each word is familiar to the students.

Procedure

1. Gather a small group of students. Distribute a "Letter Chart" to each child.
2. Draw the students' attention to the letters on the chart. Explain that each letter of the alphabet is on the chart.
3. Hold up an environmental-print word and ask the students to say its name. Then, ask the students to identify the letter at the beginning of the word.
4. Ask each child to locate that letter on the chart and cover it with a paper square or game marker.
5. Continue in this manner, showing an environmental-print word, asking the students to read it and identify the beginning letter, and covering it up on the chart.
6. Review the letters that were covered on the chart. Ask the students to think of other words they know of that begin with particular letters.

Letter Hunt (cont.)

Sample Dialog

Teacher: (Teacher holds up the word *exit*.) What does this word say?

Student: E*xit*

Teacher: What letter do you see at the beginning of the word?

Student: **E**

Teacher: Right. Exit begins with **E**. Look on your chart and find the letter **E**. When you find it, cover it up.

Student: (Students find and cover the letter.)

Teacher: Let's say the word again. This time, listen carefully to the sound that **E** makes.

Student: E*xit*—it says /e/.

Teacher: That's right. Now, let's read another word.

Assessment

Observe as the students locate the letters on their charts and identify the sounds heard at the beginnings of the words.

Differentiation

- For an added challenge, have the students identify the ending letters of words.
- Have the students locate and cut out other words from advertisements, magazines, or newspapers, creating their own collection of environmental print to use for playing the game at a learning center. (Be sure to preview any print media for appropriate content.)

Letter Chart

Letter Chart	Aa	Bb
Cc	Dd	Ee	Ff
Gg	Hh	Ii	Jj

Glue Tab

Letter Chart (cont.)

Kk	Ll	Mm	Nn
Oo	Pp	Qq	Rr
Ss	Tt	Uu	Vv
Ww	Xx	Yy	Zz

Beginning-Letter Match

Activity Format

Small group/
Independent practice

Objective

Students will match words to their beginning letters.

Materials

- eight environmental-print words (each one beginning with a different letter)
- scissors
- 16 index cards
- glue
- marker
- chart paper

Preparation

1. Cut out eight environmental-print words. (Be sure each one begins with a different letter.)
2. Glue each word to an index card.
3. Write each beginning letter on its own index card.

Procedure

1. Gather a small group of students. Display the environmental-print words and discuss the beginning letters.
2. Draw the students' attention to one of the beginning letters. Ask the students to name the letter.
3. Write that letter on chart paper. Point out that the letter at the beginning of the product name may look different from the written letter. For example, the **L** in LEGO is white, slanted, and outlined. It looks different than the **L** written on chart paper, but they are both the letter **L**.
4. Continue in this manner with the remaining words.
5. Explain to the children how to play a memory game with the word and letter cards.
6. Place the environmental-print words and letter cards facedown on a flat surface. Explain that the point of the game is to match a word card to its corresponding letter card.
7. Play the game as a small group and then place the cards at a learning center for the students to practice on their own.

Beginning–Letter Match (cont.)

Sample Dialog

Teacher: (Teacher holds up the word *Band-Aid*.) What does this word say?

Student: *Band-Aid*.

Teacher: What letter do you see at the beginning of the word?

Student: **B.**

Teacher: Right. *Band-Aid* begins with the letter **B**. Watch as I write the letter **B** on the chart. Notice that the **B** in *Band-Aid* looks a bit different from the **B** I wrote. The **B** in *Band-Aid* is red and thick. The other **B** is just black and written with a marker.

Assessment

Observe as the students identify the letter at the beginning of each word. Then, pay attention to each student's ability to recognize letters in product names that may be in a different form than standard type.

Differentiation

- For an added challenge, add more environmental-print word cards and letter cards to the set.
- Increase the difficulty level by including more environmental-print words that begin with the same letter. This will give the students the opportunity to recognize the same letter printed in different forms.

Puzzle Spelling

Activity Format

Small group

Objective

Students will assemble print puzzles by blending sounds.

Materials

- one environmental-print word to use as a sample (Step one in the procedure directions.)
- eight environmental-print words (short words with phonetic spelling)
- scissors
- puzzle card templates (pages 50–51)
- glue
- plastic zipper bags

Preparation

1. Cut out eight environmental-print words. Each word should be a short word that is phonetically spelled, such as *stop*, *on*, *off*, *exit*, *Dots*™, *Eggo*, *Jell-O*, and *Oreo*™.

2. Cut each letter of the word apart and glue the letters onto a puzzle template so the letters are in order, but in separate sections. (For words with double letters, like *off* or *Eggo*, you might choose not to cut the double letters apart.)

3. Cut the puzzle pieces apart between the letters.

Procedure

1. Gather a small group of students. Display a short phonetically spelled word, such as *stop*. Ask the students to say the name of the word.

2. Tell the students that when we read, we blend letter sounds together to make words.

3. Run your finger below each letter as you blend the letter sounds together: /s//t//o//p/

4. Next, take out the puzzle pieces for one of the words. Tell the students that they will blend sounds together to make words. For example, post **S** and say /s/. Then, post **T** and say /t/.

5. Emphasize how the sounds blend together rather than saying each one in isolation.

6. When each puzzle piece is assembled, say the whole word as a group.

7. Continue in this manner with the remaining puzzles.

Puzzle Spelling (cont.)

Sample Dialog

Teacher: (Teacher holds up the word *stop*.) What does this word say?

Student: *Stop*

Teacher: When we read, we blend sounds together. Listen as I blend the sounds together in the word *stop*. (Say /s//t//o//p/.) Let's read that again. This time, blend the sounds together with me.

Student: /s/ /t/ /o/ /p/

Teacher: I have puzzle pieces that go together to make words. Let's blend the sounds together to make words. (Display each piece one at a time while saying the letter sound aloud. Invite the students to join you.)

Assessment

Observe as the students verbalize the letter sounds. Pay attention to each student's ability to blend one letter sound into the next letter sound.

Differentiation

- Place each set of puzzle pieces in a plastic zipper bag. Then, place the puzzles at a learning center for children to assemble independently or with partners. Encourage them to blend the sounds aloud as they assemble each puzzle.
- Increase the difficulty level by including puzzles made of longer words. Avoid words that cannot be sounded out phonetically.

Puzzle Templates

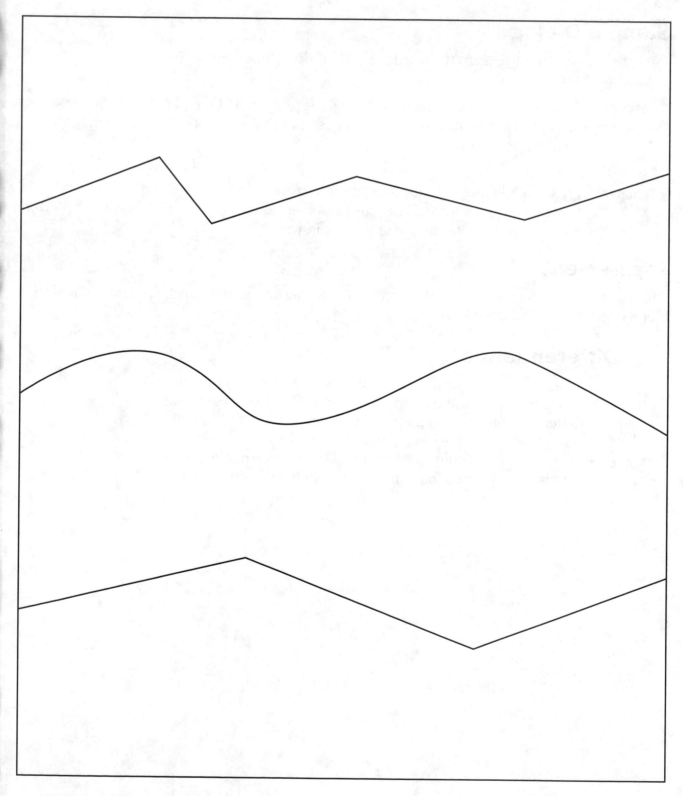

Puzzle Templates

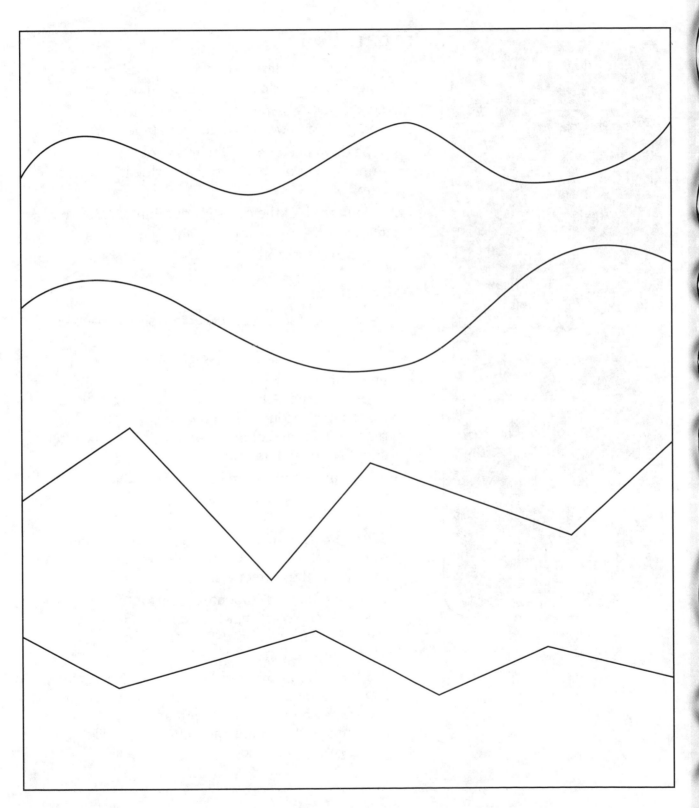

Decontextualized Reading

Activity Format

Small group

Objective

Students will read environmental-print words in varying forms to encourage transfer from whole word identification to alphabetic decoding.

Materials

- four environmental-print words in varying forms (See the preparation directions.)
- 24 index cards (for each child)
- glue
- word processor and printer
- scissors
- three plastic zipper bags

Preparation

1. Duplicate four different environmental-print words in color and glue each to a different index card.
2. Duplicate the same four words in black and white, and glue each word to a different index card.
3. Type the name of each environmental-print word. Print and cut out each word and glue it to an index card.
4. Laminate all of the cards for durability, if desired.
5. Place each set of word cards in a different plastic zipper bag for storage.

Procedure

1. Gather the students together in a small group at a table.
2. Arrange the cards in columns. For example, all environmental-print word cards in color are placed in one column. All black-and-white word cards are placed in a second column. All typed word cards are placed in a third column. Cards within each column should appear in random order.
3. Point out that there are four words on the cards, but that they are different: some are in color, some are in black and white, some are typed.
4. Say one of the words and ask a student to find it in the first column. Be sure that all the students agree that this is the correct word.
5. Then, ask another student to look for the same word in the second column. Remind the student that these are the same words, but they are in black and white.
6. Continue in this manner, asking the students to locate the same word in the column of typed words. Assist the children by asking them to listen for the beginning letter sound and determine the letter that represents that sound.

Decontextualized Reading (cont.)

Sample Dialog

Teacher: Look at the cards on the table. What do you notice about the way they look and how they are arranged?

Student: Some of the cards are in color and some aren't.

Teacher: Notice the colorful words in the first column. The second column has the same words, but they are in black and white. What do you see in the third column?

Student: The words are different. (Answers will vary.)

Teacher: Look at the first column and point to the word *Barbie*.

Student: (A selected student points to the word.)

Teacher: Now look for the word *Barbie* in the second column. Look carefully at the first letter.

Student: (A selected student points to the word.)

Teacher: Let's try to find the word in the last column. Don't let these words confuse you. Just look for a word that begins with the letter **B**.

Assessment

Observe as each student searches for and identifies environmental-print words in the columns. Determine each child's ability to recognize letters in the words where color and graphics have been removed.

Differentiation

- Increase the difficulty of this activity by creating sets of cards that have several different environmental-print words that all begin with the same letter, such as *Kraft*™ *Macaroni & Cheese*, *McDonald's*, and *M&M's*™.
- For the students who need more assistance, begin by displaying only the first column of color words and asking the students to identify them. Progress to the black-and-white words if appropriate.

Sounding out Words

Activity Format

Small group

Objective

Students will identify the sounds made by the letters in order to decode words.

Materials

- "Word Chart" (page 56)
- a supply of environmental-print words (See the preparation directions.)
- scissors
- tape

Preparation

1. Collect familiar environmental-print words. Create one set in color, one set in black and white, and one set typed. (See the preparation directions on page 52.) Laminate the environmental-print words for durability, if desired.
2. Duplicate the "Word Chart." Laminate the chart.

Procedure

1. Work with the children in small groups.
2. Display an environmental-print word in color for the students. Tape it in the first square of the first column on the Word Chart. Point to one letter at a time and ask the students to identify the name of the letter.
3. Then, ask the students to identify the sound made by each letter.
4. Explain that when reading, we say each letter sound and blend it into the next. Try this with a word, such as *Disney*. Assist the students in blending the letter sounds together to decode the word—/d//i//s//n//e/
5. Show the students how to slowly blend the letters and then blend the sounds even more, connecting the sounds to make the word.
6. Show the students the black-and-white version of the word. Point out that the two words are the same, but that one is in black and white. Tape the word below the second column on the chart.
7. Then, tape the typed version of the word to the last column on the chart. Show the students that the letters are the same and that they are sounded out in the same manner.
8. Continue in this manner with several of the words.

Sounding out Words (cont.)

Sample Dialog

Teacher: (Teacher displays the colored word *Jell-O*.) When reading a word, we say each letter sound and blend them together. Let's try blending these letter sounds together. (Point to each letter while blending.)

Student: /j//e//l//o/

Teacher: What word does /j//e//l//o/ spell?

Student: *Jell-O*

Teacher: That's great! Now, let's look at the typed word *Jell-O*. Notice that the letters are the same. How are these letters different from the first word?

Student: They are not in color. They are smaller. They are black.

Assessment

Determine each child's ability to identify letter sounds and blend them together to say a word. Record each correctly blended word.

Differentiation

- Ask the students to identify the beginning letter and sound.
- For a more challenging activity, provide each child in the group with a different environmental-print word. Ask each student to identify the sounds in the word and then decode the word for the other group members.
- For a greater challenge, provide the students with typed words to sound out and read.

Word Chart

Color	Black and White	Typed

Identifying Blends

Activity Format

Whole group

Objective

Students will identify and sort words by blends.

Materials

- a supply of environmental-print words (beginning with selected blends, such as **fr, tr, st**)
- three library pockets
- poster board
- glue
- marker
- scissors

Preparation

1. Glue three library pockets to a piece of poster board.
2. Select three digraphs as the focus of the lesson. Then, cut out a picture of an object that begins with each blend. For example, you might select a frog, a truck, and stairs. Glue a picture to the front of each pocket.
3. Prepare a set of environmental-print words. (The words should begin with the three blends selected.) Environmental print can be cut from newspaper ads, product packaging, and coupons, or printed from the computer, such as *Fritos, Froot Loops, Frosted Flakes*™, *Trix, Triscuit*™, *Sesame Street, Stop, Starburst*™
4. Laminate the environmental-print words for durability, if desired.

Procedure

1. Gather the students together. Show the students the pocket board. Ask the students to identify each picture on the pocket board. Point out that the sound at the beginning of each is a blend of two letter sounds.
2. Review each blend and the sound it makes.
3. Show the students one of the selected environmental-print words. Say the word slowly, emphasizing the blend sound.
4. Ask the students to identify which blend on the pocket board has the same beginning sound as the blend in the word.
5. When the word is matched to a picture, place the word in the corresponding pocket.
6. Continue in this manner with the remaining environmental-print words.

Identifying Blends (cont.)

Sample Dialog

Teacher: What picture do you see on this pocket?

Student: *Stairs*.

Teacher: Let's listen to the sound at the beginning of *stairs*. (Emphasize the /st/ sound.) What sound do you hear? (Encourage the students to identify the sound rather than the letter.)

Student: /st/

Teacher: Yes, *stairs* begins with the /st/ sound. (Do the same with the two other pictures.)

Teacher: Look at this word (*Sesame Street*). Look at the word *street*. What blend do you hear at the beginning of the word?

Student: /st/

Teacher: Which picture has the same beginning blend?

Student: *Stairs*.

Assessment

Observe the students' participation during the activity. Pay attention to the students' abilities to identify the blends at the beginnings of the words. If necessary, take extra time to emphasize the beginning sounds.

Differentiation

- Place the materials at a learning center and encourage the students to sort words independently.
- Conduct a similar activity, using consonant digraphs (**th**, **wh**, **sh**, and **ch**) rather than blends.

Long Vowels or Short Vowels

Activity Format

Whole group

Objective

Students will identify the vowel sounds and sort words by short or long vowel sounds.

Materials

- a supply of environmental-print words (all should have same vowel—some long, some short)
- sheet of construction paper
- marker
- scissors
- tape (or other temporary adhesive)

Preparation

1. Fold the sheet of construction paper in half. Use the marker to write *Short* A on one side and *Long* A on the other.

2. Prepare a set of environmental-print words—half the words should have short vowels and half should have long vowels. See below.

   Short A Words: *Apple Jacks*™, *Campbell's*™ (*soup*), (*Golden*) *Grahams*™

   Long A Words: *Lay's* (*potato chips*), *Play-*(*Doh*), (*Frosted*) *Flakes*, *Raisin* (*Bran*)™

3. Laminate the environmental-print words for durability, if desired.

Procedure

1. Gather the students together. Display the construction paper labeled with Short A and Long A. Ask the students to identify the sound of short **a**. Then, ask the students to think of words they know that have the short **a** sound (*cat, lamp, trample*).

2. Next, ask the students to identify the sound of long **a**. Ask the students to think of words they know that have the long **a** sound (*stay, gate, same*).

3. Tell the students that they will be asked to read a set of words. Their job is to identify the words that have the long **a** sound and those that have the short **a** sound.

4. One at a time, hold up an environmental-print word. Ask the students to say the word. Then, repeat the word, emphasizing the featured vowel sound. Tape each word on the construction paper below the corresponding label. (Some words are likely to have more than one vowel sound. In these cases, focus the students on the letter **a**.)

5. Continue in this manner with the remaining environmental-print words.

Long Vowels or Short Vowels (cont.)

Sample Dialog

Teacher: What is this word?

Student: *Play-Doh*

Teacher: I'm going to say the word again. Listen to the sound you hear in *play*. (Emphasize the long **a** sound.) What sound do you hear? (Encourage the students to identify the sound rather than the letter.)

Student: **A**

Teacher: Is that a short **a** or long **a**?

Student: Long **A**

Teacher: Yes, the **a** in *Play-Doh* is a long **A**.

Assessment

Observe the students' participation during the activity. Pay attention to students' abilities to identify the vowel sounds in the words. If necessary, take extra time to emphasize the ending sounds.

Differentiation

- Conduct the same activity focusing on a different vowel sound.
- Place the materials at a learning center and encourage the students to repeat the activity independently.
- Challenge the students to bring in environmental-print words from home that have different long and short vowel sounds.

CVC Words

Preparation

1. Prepare a set of environmental-print words to use for the activity. The environmental-print words should all have at least one word that has the CVC pattern. Examples include:

   Dots, Jif™, *(Jack in the) Box*™, *Kit Kat, Kix, (Corn) Pops*

2. Laminate the environmental-print words for durability, if desired.

Procedure

1. Gather the students together. Write the word *cat* on the board.

2. Draw the students' attention to the letters in the word. Point out that **c** is a consonant, **a** is a vowel, and **t** is a consonant. Explain that many words have this pattern, and when reading a CVC word, the vowel usually makes a short sound.

3. Provide a few more examples to the students, such as *ham*, *tip*, *mom*, etc.

4. Next, hold up one of the environmental-print words, such as *Jif*.

5. Ask the students to listen carefully to the word as you say it again. Ask the students to look carefully at the letters and decide which are vowels and which are consonants. Draw their attention to the CVC pattern.

6. Try this activity again with another CVC environmental-print word.

7. Continue in this manner with the remaining environmental-print words. If a CVC word ends with the letter **s,** cover it up to draw attention to the root word.

CVC Words (cont.)

Sample Dialog

Teacher: (Hold up the J*if* label.) What does this word say?

Student: J*if*!

Teacher: Let's look closely at the letters in J*if*. Is **j** a consonant or a vowel?

Student: Consonant.

Teacher: (Teacher writes **c** on the board.) That's right. **j** is a consonant. Is **i** a consonant or a vowel?

Student: Vowel.

Teacher: (Teacher writes **v** for vowel on the board.) What kind of letter is **f**?

Student: Consonant!

Teacher: (Teacher writes **c** on the board.) Great! Does J*if* follow the CVC pattern?

Student: Yes!

Assessment

Observe the students' active participation during the activity. Each student should have the opportunity to identify consonants and vowels in words.

Differentiation

- Challenge the students by having them identify CVC words in other printed material they look at. Collect other examples and place them in a CVC booklet or post them on a word wall.
- Conduct the same activity with a small group of students. Have the students practice identifying consonants and vowels in environmental-print words and in other words.
- Students who struggle with this skill may need to focus on individual consonants or vowels rather than looking for CVC patterns in whole words.

R-Controlled Vowels

Activity Format

Whole group

Objective

Students will identify the sounds of words with r-controlled vowels.

Materials

- "R-Controlled Vowels Chart" (page 65)
- a supply of environmental-print words
- chalkboard and chalk (or whiteboard and markers)
- scissors
- glue

Preparation

1. Prepare a set of familiar environmental-print words to use for the activity. The environmental-print words should all have r-controlled vowels in them. See the examples below.

ar	er	ir	or	ur
Arby's	Burger King	Miracle Whip™	Doritos	Burger King
Arthur			Oreo	
Barbie	Life Savers			Starburst
Barney				
Starburst				
Wal-Mart™				

2. Laminate the environmental-print words and category labels for durability, if desired.

Procedure

1. Gather the students together. Write the letters **ar**, **er**, **ir**, **or**, and **ur** on the board. Point out that each of these has a vowel followed by an **r**. Words with these letter pairs are called r-controlled because the **r** changes the sound of the vowel.

2. Say the sound of each letter pair and ask the students to repeat the sound.

3. Then, display an environmental-print word, such as *Wal-Mart*. Ask the students to identify the vowel with **r** in that word.

4. Continue in this manner with the remaining environmental-print words.

5. Review each of the words again and ask the students to tell the sound made by the vowel with **r**.

6. For additional practice, duplicate the "R-Controlled Vowels Chart" and have the students glue the words in the corresponding columns.

R-Controlled Vowels (cont.)

Sample Dialog

Teacher:	What is this word? (Teacher holds up *Wal-Mart*.)
Student:	*Wal-Mart!*
Teacher:	Right. Who can find the vowel with **r** in this word?
Student:	(One student points to **ar**.)
Teacher:	What sound does **ar** make in the word *Wal-Mart*? Let's look at another **ar** word to see if the sound is the same.
Teacher:	(Teacher holds up *Arthur*.) Find the **ar** in *Arthur*. Say the word with me and listen closely.
Student:	*Arthur*
Teacher:	Does the **ar** in *Wal-Mart* (emphasize the /är/ sound the same as the **ar** in *Arthur*?
Student:	Yes!

Assessment

Observe the students' participation during the activity. Allow each student the opportunity to identify the sounds of r-controlled vowels by saying them aloud to a partner.

Differentiation

- On the wall, post labels with **ar**, **er**, **ir**, **or**, and **ur**. Encourage the students to bring in environmental-print words that have r-controlled vowels and post them below the corresponding labels.
- On the wall, post labels with **ar**, **er**, **ir**, **or**, and **ur**. Place a basket of environmental-print words with r-controlled vowels near the labels. Have the students tape the words below the corresponding labels.
- For an added challenge, ask the students to think of other words with r-controlled vowels and write them on paper.

R-Controlled Vowels Chart

R-Controlled Vowels Chart	ur	
	or	
	ir	
	er	
ar		

Fluency and Comprehension

There are many effective ways to use environmental print to build fluency and to develop comprehension skills. Interaction with print that is high profile and familiar to students creates an excellent cognitive anchor for making sense while reading.

Fluency

Fluency is the ability to read quickly and accurately while at the same time using good oral expression, proper phrasing, and appropriate pacing. Fluency is particularly important when considering young children who are just learning to read or struggling readers, or children learning English as a second language. These students expend too much cognitive energy decoding words letter by letter, losing understanding of the material. Their attention and energy is focused on getting each sound correct rather than finding meaning and making sense of the text. This is clear when, after listening to a struggling reader, the student does not understand what has just been read. Children who read more fluently use their cognitive energy and attention to focus on the meaning of the print. They comprehend what they read. The fluent reader has enough attention in reserve to make connections between the text and their own background knowledge, which gives the reader a deeper understanding of the material. When oral reading of text is more fluent and sounds like natural speech, children are better able to pull from their own prior knowledge and background experiences for comprehension.

Building Comprehension

Good readers are taught to use a wide array of strategies to make sense of what they are reading. They are explicitly taught to make connections as they read by using their prior knowledge and visualizing, inferring, and synthesizing skills. Good readers ask questions before they read, as they read, and after they read. Street signs, cereal boxes, and billboards all provide opportunities for readers to interact with words in a meaningful, purposeful way.

This section provides a variety of lessons and activities that will assist you with creative ideas for repeated readings for building fluency and developing comprehension. The lessons in this section are designed to look beyond the color and context clues of environmental print to read words. Provided are a variety of writing activities and ways to reinforce making meaning during reading, as well as ways to scaffold the development of comprehension strategies.

Environmental-Print Word Wall

Activity Format

Whole group

Objective

Students will develop word recognition and fluency by identifying and reading familiar print in the environment from a classroom word wall.

Materials

- one each of 26 letters of the alphabet
- index cards for recording new word wall words
- glue or glue stick
- tape, stapler, or pushpins for new word cards

Preparation

1. Cut out or die cut one each of the 26 letters of the alphabet for word wall headings. Laminate the letter headings for durability, if desired.

2. Staple, pin, or tape the letters of the alphabet in order on a bulletin board or wall space to serve as headings to group newly learned words together.

3. Before the lesson, direct students to collect packaging, containers, etc., from home which have printed words they know and can read. Alternately, have a prepared set of environmental-print words from newspaper ads or product packaging, or printed from the computer. Be certain to have some packaging for those students who forget or are unable to bring words into class.

Procedure

1. Gather the students together. Show the students an environmental-print word that you have chosen as an example. Draw the students' attention to the starting letter of the word.

2. Ask the students which letter on the word wall corresponds with the beginning letter of the sample word.

3. Read the word with the whole class. Glue the word onto an index card and attach the card to the word wall underneath the appropriate letter heading.

4. Continue reviewing each word that students have gathered in the same manner. Have the students read the environmental-print words and identify under which letters of the word wall the words should be posted

5. When all words have been posted on the word wall, read each column of words chorally as a whole group.

6. Continue this activity as students find more environmental-print words, signs, and packaging to bring into class.

Environmental–Print Word Wall (cont.)

Sample Dialog

Teacher: This is my favorite flavor of gum. Does anyone know the word that is printed on my gum package?

Student: I do! It's Doublemint™.

Teacher: Yes, it is. Everyone read this name together with me. "Doublemint" What is the first letter on the name of my favorite gum?

Students: **D**

Teacher: Look at the alphabet that I have posted on the wall near our library center. That is a word wall that we are going to fill up together with new words that we are learning. Can you find the **D** on our word wall?

Student: It comes after **C**, right here!

Teacher: Correct! I am going to glue my Doublemint wrapper on to this card and then put the card up under the letter **D** because that is the letter that my word begins with. Now, what things did you bring in that are your favorites?

Assessment

Observe the students' participation during this activity. Pay close attention to the students' alphabet knowledge. Using a class list as a checklist, mark off those who bring in environmental-print words as well as those who have the alphabet knowledge required.

Differentiation

- Conduct the same activity using a manuscript decontextualized version of the word for the word wall
- Conduct the same activity with a small group of students.
- Conduct the same activity using other new vocabulary words, student names, and sight words.

Word Wall Reading Sponge Activities

Activity Format
Whole group

Objective
Students will read and reread words on the word wall for increased fluency and word recognition.

Materials
- word wall

Preparation
1. Follow the directions to create an Environmental-Print Word Wall (page 67).

Procedure
1. During transition times when sponge activities are helpful, have the students chorally read columns of words from the word wall.

2. Alternately, have groups of students chorally read columns of words from the word wall. Change the grouping pattern with each new column, challenging the groups to "race" for speed and accuracy. Groups can be organized by boys and girls, table groups, rows, birthdays, clothing, or eye or hair color.

3. Play "I Spy" with the word wall. (See the Sample Dialog.)

4. Have students create sentences using environmental-print words from the word wall.

5. Spell environmental-print words from the word wall chorally.

6. For continued development of phonological awareness, rhyme the environmental-print words on the word wall with other words. For example, *Trix* rhymes with *Twix*, sticks, picks, six, etc.

7. Play "I went walking and I saw . . ." reading and rereading words that begin with the same letter. The teacher sets the pattern for the class. Students then take turns adding a new environmental-print word to the chant.

    I went walking and I saw *Taco Bell*.

    I went walking and I saw *Toys "R" Us* and *Taco Bell*.

    I went walking and I saw a *Tootsie Roll*, *Toys "R" Us*, and *Taco Bell*.

    I went walking and I saw *Trix*, a *Tootsie Roll*, *Toys "R" Us*, and *Taco Bell*.

Word Wall Reading Sponge Activities (cont.)

Sample Dialog

Teacher: I spy with my little eye a word on our word wall that rhymes with *poke*.

Students: *Coke™*.

Teacher: I spy with my little eye a word on our word wall that names my favorite gum.

Students: *Doublemint*.

Teacher: I spy with my little eye a word on our word wall that is a kind of bandage.

Students: *Band-Aid*.

Teacher: I spy with my little eye a word on the word wall that is a type of cereal.

Students: *Cheerios*.

Students: *Froot Loops*.

Students: *Frosted Flakes*.

Assessment

Observe the students' participation during the activity.

Differentiation

- Challenge the students to direct the activity by identifying words with their own "I spy with my little eye" question. The student who responds to the "I spy" question asks the next "I spy" question.
- Challenge the students by having the students write down their answers to the "I spy" questions.

Environmental-Print ABC Big Book

Activity Format

Small group

Objective

Students will read words and add them to a class-created alphabet book.

Materials

- a supply of environmental-print words
- large cardstock or heavy brown paper wrap
- glue
- scissors

Preparation

1. Prepare a set of familiar environmental-print words to use for the activity. Environmental print can be cut from newspaper ads, product packaging, and coupons, or printed from the computer. Keep in mind that environmental print also consists of functional print, such as the name of your school, a stop sign, or an exit sign.

2. Use 15 pages of cardstock for an alphabet book. Label each side of the pages in order with a single letter of the alphabet and create a front and back cover. Bind the pages at the conclusion of the activity to create the book.

Procedure

1. Gather the students together into a small group. Show them the alphabet book. Explain that the class will be creating an alphabet book from the new environmental print that they can read.

2. Spread the environmental-print words on the table.

3. Select an environmental-print word and hold it up for the students to read. Draw attention to the beginning letter of the word. Decide with the students on which page of the book the word should be placed.

4. Glue the word in the alphabet book.

5. Ask students to look at the other words on the table and find any other words that should be glued to the same page.

6. Ask the students to continue matching words to the alphabet pages.

7. Have the students read the pages either one at a time or as a whole group as the group time ends.

Environmental-Print ABC Big Book (cont.)

Sample Dialog

Teacher:	What is this word?
Students:	*Barney.*
Teacher:	What is the beginning letter in the word *Barney*?
Students:	**B**
Teacher:	Yes, let's glue *Barney* to the letter **B** page.
Teacher:	Can you find any other words that begin with **B**?
Students:	*Barbie.*
Students:	Here is *Burger King.*
Teacher:	That's right. Glue the words that you just found on to the **B** page of our alphabet book. Remember—use just a dot of glue so that it dries quickly.

(Students glue the words on to the pages.)

Teacher: Let's read the **B** words together that we found for our ABC book.

Assessment

Observe the students' participation in the group. Pay attention to the students' letter-recognition skills. Use a class list as a checklist to note which letters individual students have mastered. If necessary, take extra time to emphasize the letter names.

Differentiation

- Place the materials at a learning center and encourage the students to repeat the activity independently with other letter pages.
- Conduct the same activity with students searching through advertisements, magazines, or newspapers to find their own words for the alphabet book pages. (Be sure to preview any print media for appropriate content.)
- Conduct the same activity with a small group of students using student names and sight words to be included in the ABC book.
- Read and reread the words in varying groups and patterns. For example, boys and girls can alternate reading; read slowly; read quickly; read softly; read loudly.
- Place the completed book in the classroom library for independent reading.

Environmental-Print ABC Little Book

Activity Format

Small group

Objective

Students will read and sort words by the beginning letter to complete a little alphabet book.

Materials

- "ABC Little Book Template" (pages 75–81)
- a supply of environmental-print words
- glue
- stapler
- scissors

Preparation

1. Prepare a set of environmental-print words to use for the activity.
2. Photocopy the "ABC Little Book Templates." Make one copy for each student.
3. Fold each of the seven pages in half by width and again lengthwise. (For the first page, **Aa** and **Bb** will be on the inside folds, and the title and the letter **Cc** will be on the outside folds.)
4. Place the folded pages together and staple.

Procedure

1. Gather the students together. Show them a little alphabet book. Explain that each student will be creating his or her very own alphabet book from the new environmental-print words and signs that he or she can read.
2. Spread out the environmental-print words on the table.
3. Select an environmental-print word and hold it up for the students to read. Draw attention to the beginning letter of the word. Decide with the students on which page of the book the word should be placed.
4. Glue the word on the correct page of the alphabet book.
5. Ask the students to continue looking through the environmental-print words on the table for other words that begin with that letter.
6. Glue the words in the alphabet book.
7. Ask the students to continue matching words to the little alphabet book.
8. Have the students read the pages of their little alphabet books to partners.

Environmental–Print ABC Little Book (cont.)

Sample Dialog

Teacher: What word is this?

Students: *Cheerios.*

Teacher: What is the beginning letter in the word *Cheerios*?

Students: **C**

Teacher: That's right. Let's find the **Cc** page in the alphabet book and glue the word *Cheerios* on that page. (Glue the word in the alphabet book.)

Teacher: Look through the other words on the table. Can you find any other words that begin with the letter **C**?

Students: *Coke.*

Students: Here is *Cocoa Puffs*™.

Students: CVS™ drugstore starts with **C**, too.

Teacher: That's right. Go ahead and glue the words that you just found onto the **Cc** page in your little alphabet book. Remember—use just a dot of glue so that it dries quickly.

(Students glue the words on to the pages.)

Assessment

Observe the students' participation in the group. Pay attention to the students' letter-recognition skills. Use a class list as a checklist to note which letters individual students have mastered. If necessary, take extra time to emphasize the letter names on the letters that the students have not mastered.

Differentiation

- Have the students work independently on completing the ABC little book.
- Have the students write the words from environmental print into their ABC book rather than glue the environmental print into the book.
- Conduct the same activity with students searching through advertising or magazines independently to find their own words for the little alphabet book pages. (Be sure to preview any print media for appropriate content.)
- Conduct the same activity with a small group of students, using student names and sight words to be included in the ABC book.

ABC Little Book Template

Cc

Student Name
_____

My ABC Book

Aa

Bb

ABC Little Book Template (cont.)

Dd	Gg
Ee	Ff

ABC Little Book Template (cont.)

Hh

Kk

Ii

Jj

ABC Little Book Template (cont.)

Ll	Oo
Mm	Nn

ABC Little Book Template (cont.)

Pp

Ss

Qq

Rr

A BC Little Book Template (cont.)

Tt	Ww
Uu	Vv

ABC Little Book Template (cont.)

Xx

The End

Yy

Zz

Writing with Environmental Print

Activity Format

Small group

Objective

Students will select and read environmental-print words to create an original book.

Materials

- a supply of environmental-print words
- large construction paper
- glue
- scissors
- pencils or markers

Preparation

1. Create blank little books from large construction paper, one book per student. Fold large construction paper in half lengthwise. Then, fold the paper in half and in half again so that three folds create four pages. For more pages, staple a spine on the left side of the accordion book, then cleanly the trim top, bottom, and right edges.

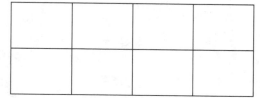

2. Prepare a set of familiar environmental-print words to use for the activity. Environmental print can be cut from newspaper ads, product packaging, and coupons, or printed from the computer. Multiple copies of some words may be needed if children choose the same word. For example, *McDonald's* is a popular, frequently chosen word for this activity.

3. Make a sample blank book by gluing a different word onto each page. Write a caption for the word you have glued into the book. For example, a Pepsi caption might read "My favorite soda is Pepsi."

Procedure

1. Gather students together into a small group.

2. Show the students your sample book and explain that they will create their own original books. Also, explain that they will be able to choose the words they want in their books and create the text for each page.

3. Have students read the environmental-print words aloud and decide which words would be best for their own books. Give each student his or her own blank book.

4. After the students have selected and glued the words into the book pages, encourage them to begin writing the accompanying sentences for each page.

5. Use this activity as an occasion for a writing conference by providing mini-lessons and reinforcement of writing conventions.

6. Direct students to read their completed books aloud to a partner.

Writing with Environmental Print (cont.)

Sample Dialog

Teacher: What is this word that you have chosen for your book?

Student: LEGO

Teacher: Yes. Why did you choose LEGO for your book?

Student: I love to play with my LEGOs. I have all the LEGO sets at my house.

Teacher: What would you like to write in your book about LEGOs?

Student: I am going to write "My favorite LEGO set is the pirate island."

Teacher: All right, then, what is the first word of your sentence?

Student: My

Teacher: Good! Write My. How do you always begin a sentence?

Student: With a capital letter, so I start with a capital **M**.

Teacher: You've got it. You can finish writing the sentence.

Assessment

Observe the students' participation during the activity. Assess written product for stage of writing development and fine motor control.

Differentiation

- The students can work independently or in small groups once they start their work on this activity.
- For students who need an added challenge, ask them to write more than one sentence.
- For an additional challenge, have the students include a specific concept in their books. For example, they must create a page for each day of the week.

Fluency and Comprehension

Writing a Personal "My Letter Book" with Environmental Print

Activity Format

Small group

Objective

Students will create books using environmental print that begins with the first letters of their names.

Materials

- "Letter Book Cover Template" (page 86)
- a supply of environmental-print words
- large construction paper
- glue
- scissors
- pencils or markers

Preparation

1. Create blank books from the large construction paper, one book per student, by folding large construction paper lengthwise once. Then, fold the paper in half and in half again so that the three folds create six width-wise pages. For more pages, staple a spine on the left side of the accordion book, and then cleanly trim top, bottom, and right edges.

2. Photocopy, cut out, and glue the cover template on the front of each blank book.

3. Prepare a set of environmental-print words for the activity. Environmental print can be cut from newspaper ads, product packaging, and coupons, or printed from the computer.

4. Review the names on your class list for the most commonly appearing first initial as you collect the environmental-print words.

Procedure

1. Gather students together into a small group.

2. Show the students the blank books and explain that each student will create his or her own original letter books. Students' letter books will be filled with words that begin with the beginning letter of their names. Also, explain that they will be able to choose the words that begin with the beginning letter of their names, and they will be able to create the text for each page. Give each student his or her own blank book.

3. Have the students review the environmental-print words and decide what words would be best for their letter books.

4. After students have selected and glued their words into their book pages, encourage them to begin writing accompanying sentences for each page. For example, Jimmy juggles Jelly Bellies.

5. Use this activity as an occasion for a writing conference by providing mini-lessons and reinforcement of writing conventions.

6. Direct students to read their completed books aloud to partners. Have partners exchange their letter books and read.

Writing a Personal "My Letter Book" with Environmental Print (cont.)

Sample Dialog

Teacher:	What is the first letter of Jimmy's name?
Student:	**J**
Teacher:	Right. What are the other words that are in Jimmy's letter book?
Students:	*Jelly Belly, Jif* peanut butter, *Jack in the Box, Juicy Juice*™, *Juicy Fruit*™ gum, *Jujubes*™
Teacher:	Listen carefully as I read the sentence in Jimmy's book that is on the Jack in the Box page—*Jimmy jumps for joy at Jack in the Box.* What sounds do you hear in this sentence from Jimmy's letter book?
Student:	I hear /j/.
Teacher:	All right! Listen to the next page carefully for the /j/ sound. *Jimmy chews juicy Juicy Fruit.* What words in that sentence have the /j/ sound?
Student:	*Juicy.*
Student:	*Juicy Fruit.*
Teacher:	You've got it.

Assessment

Observe the students' participation during the activity. Assess the written product for stage of writing development and fine motor control.

Differentiation

- Students can work independently once the activity has been started.
- For students who need an added challenge, ask them to write more than one sentence per page for each caption.

Letter Book Cover Template

_____**'s**

Letter Book

_____**'s**

Letter Book

#50049—Reading Is All Around Us   © *Shell Education*

Pattern Book with Environmental Print

Activity Format

Whole group

Objective

Students will read and reread an original pattern Book for word recognition and fluency.

Materials

- "Pattern Book Templates" (pages 89–102)
- a supply of environmental-print words
- glue
- pencils or markers
- scissors

Preparation

1. Select a pattern book and duplicate a set of the templates from the templates provided. Alternately, you may create an original pattern for students to use. Staple the set of pages into a book, one for each student.

2. Prepare a set of environmental-print words to use for the activity. Environmental print can be cut from newspaper ads, product packaging, and coupons, or printed from the computer. Multiple copies of some words may be needed if children choose the same word. For example, *McDonald's* is a popular, frequently chosen word for this activity.

3. Make a sample pattern book by gluing a different environmental-print word on to each page. Complete the caption for the word you have glued into the book. For example, the pattern of "At the store, we buy_____." might be completed with environmental-print words such as *Band-Aids*, *Cheerios*, *Jif Peanut Butter*, etc.

Procedure

1. Gather the students together.

2. Show the students your sample book and explain that each student will be creating his or her own original book. Also, explain that students will be able to choose the words they want in their books, and they will be able to complete the caption for each page.

3. Have the students read environmental-print words aloud and decide what words would be best for their own books. Give each student his or her own pattern book.

4. After the students have selected and glued their words into their book pages, have them complete the patterned caption by writing in the name from the environmental-print word.

5. Use this activity as an occasion for a writing conference by providing mini-lessons and reinforcement of writing conventions.

6. Direct the students to read and reread their completed books aloud to partners.

Pattern Book with Environmental Print (cont.)

Sample Dialog

Teacher:	What is this word that you have chosen for your book?
Student:	*Safeway*™.
Teacher:	Right. Good reading! Why did you choose the word *Safeway* for your book?
Student:	My grandma and I go shopping at Safeway.
Teacher:	Go ahead and write the word *Safeway* to complete the sentence on this page of your book.
Student:	OK. (Student begins to copy the word *Safeway* into the sentence pattern.)
Teacher:	All right, then, why is the first letter of this word capital **S**?
Student:	Because it is the name of the store.
Teacher:	And what words start with a capital letter like *Safeway*?
Student:	Words that are names and places and things.
Teacher:	You've got it.

Assessment

Observe each student's ability to copy environmental-print words into the patterned sentence caption. Have the students read the book aloud to you. Listen for speed and accuracy as the students read.

Differentiation

- Conduct the same activity with a small group of students. Provide assistance to students who struggle with the identification of letter sounds.
- Photocopy an assortment of different patterned sentences to make up one book.
- Increase the number of pages in the book.

Pattern Book Templates

My Shopping Book

Name_____

My Shopping Book

Name_____

Pattern Book Templates (cont.)

At the store, we buy _____.

At the store, we buy _____.

Pattern Book Templates (cont.)

We go shopping at _____.

We go shopping at _____.

Pattern Book Templates (cont.)

My Breakfast Book

Name _____

On Monday, I ate _____
for breakfast.

Pattern Book Templates (cont.)

On Tuesday, I ate _____
for breakfast.

On Wednesday, I ate _____
for breakfast.

Pattern Book Templates (cont.)

On Thursday, I ate _____
for breakfast.

On Friday, I ate _____
for breakfast.

Pattern Book Templates (cont.)

On Saturday, I ate _____
for breakfast.

On Sunday, I ate _____
for breakfast.

Pattern Book Templates (cont.)

My Lunch Book

Name _____

I ate _____ for lunch
on Monday.

 #50049—Reading Is All Around Us

Pattern Book Templates (cont.)

I ate _____ for lunch on Tuesday.

I ate _____ for lunch on Wednesday.

Pattern Book Templates (cont.)

I ate _____ for lunch

on Thursday.

I ate _____ for lunch

on Friday.

Pattern Book Templates (cont.)

I ate _____ for lunch on Saturday.

I ate _____ for lunch on Sunday.

Pattern Book Templates (cont.)

My Food Book

Name _____

I like to eat _____.

Pattern Book Templates (cont.)

My Book

Name _____

I like _____.

Pattern Book Templates (cont.)

My Book

Name _____

Let's go to _____.

Rebus Reading in a Morning Message

Preparation

1. Prepare a set of environmental-print words to use for the activity. Environmental print can be cut from newspaper ads, product packaging, and coupons, or printed from the computer. Multiple copies of some words may be needed. For example, *McDonald's* is a popular, frequently chosen word for this activity.

2. Create a morning message for the class to read. For example, the rebus morning message might read, "This morning I had breakfast at Dunkin' Donuts™. I have Goldfish™ crackers and V8™ fruit juice for our snack this morning. How many juice boxes should I have so that each one of you gets a V8? There are new LEGOs in the block center. The cafeteria has Oreo cookies and Sun-Maid™ raisins for lunch. Do you like these snacks?" Labels for *Goldfish* crackers, V8 juice, *Dunkin' Donuts*, LEGO, *Oreo*, and *Sun-Maid* raisins should be in place of those words in the rebus morning message.

Procedure

1. Gather the students together. Show them the rebus message that you have created with the environmental-print words. Read it aloud once to the students.

2. Ask the students what they notice about the message. If necessary, say the environmental-print words slowly and focus their attention by pointing to each word of the message as you read it. This tracking is important to connect each spoken word to the written word.

3. Tell the class that rebus sentences are like puzzles where pictures represent some of the words in the sentence. Ask them to identify the "puzzle" portion of your message.

4. Ask the students to answer the questions in the message for you.

5. Have the students chorally read and reread the rebus message.

Rebus Reading in a Morning Message (cont.)

Sample Dialog Subhead

Teacher: Boys and girls, look at this chart. I have written a special kind of message to you on it. Watch carefully as I read and point to the words.

(Teacher reads the rebus sentence using a pointer or a finger to show each word.)

"This morning I had breakfast at Dunkin' Donuts. I have Goldfish crackers and V8 fruit juice for our snack this morning. How many juice boxes should I have so that each one of you gets a V8? There are new LEGOs in the block center. The cafeteria has Oreo cookies and Sun-Maid raisins for lunch. Do you like these snacks?"

Teacher: What do you notice that is very different about the sentences that I have written?

Students: They have those picture words in it. You didn't write all the words yourself.

Teacher: Exactly! These are like puzzle sentences. It is a rebus message where pictures represent some of the words in the message. Where are the rebus words in my message?

Students: *Fishy crackers . . . Goldfish* is one of those words!

Teacher: Yes. Are there any other rebus words in my sentence?

Students: V8 juice

Teacher: Correct! Are there any more?

Students: Yes!! There is *Dunkin' Donuts!*

Assessment

Observe each student's active participation and ability to read the words.

Differentiation

- Use this opportunity to reteach writing conventions by omitting periods, using only lower case, or omitting words in the morning message. Ask the students to help you edit the message.
- Place the message at a learning center and have the students read the message to each other independently.
- For a challenge, ask the students to write their own message to friends or family.
- For a challenge, remove the rebus words and have the children replace the pictures with words.

Rebus Language Experience with Environmental Print

Activity Format

Whole group

Objective

Students will read and write a rebus class message using environmental print in the place of some story words.

Materials

- a supply of environmental-print words
- glue
- paper
- chalkboard or whiteboard or chart paper
- scissors
- chalk or markers

Preparation

1. Prepare a set of environmental-print words to use for the activity. Environmental print can be cut from newspaper ads, product packaging, and coupons, or printed from the computer. Multiple copies of some words may be needed. For example, *McDonald's* is a popular, frequently chosen word for this activity.

2. Create one rebus sentence as an example for the class at the chalkboard or whiteboard or on chart paper. For example, the rebus sentence might read, "We had Goldfish crackers and V8 fruit juice for our snack this morning." Product labels for *Goldfish* crackers and V8 juice should be in place of those words in the rebus sentence.

Procedure

1. Gather the students together. Show them the rebus sentence that you have created with the environmental-print words. Read it aloud once to the students.

2. Ask the students what they notice about the sentence. If necessary, say the environmental-print words slowly and draw their attention by pointing to each word of the sentence as you read. This tracking is important to connect each spoken word to the written word.

3. Tell the class that rebus sentences are like puzzles where pictures represent some of the words in the sentence. Ask them to identify the "puzzle" portion of your sample sentence.

4. Ask the students to reread your sample sentence with you aloud.

5. Have the children brainstorm ideas of what you could write next to continue the story/message.

6. Continue by writing what the students offer including the environmental-print words that will be in the message.

7. Have students chorally read and reread their finished rebus message.

Rebus Language Experience with Environmental Print (cont.)

Sample Dialog

Teacher: Boys and girls, look at this chart. I have written a special kind of message to you on it. Watch carefully as I read and point to the sentence. (Teacher reads the rebus sentence using a pointer or a finger to show each word as it is read.) "We had Goldfish crackers and V8 fruit juice for our snack this morning."

Teacher: What do you notice is very different about this sentence that I have written?

Students: It has those picture words in it. You didn't write all the words yourself.

Teacher: Exactly! This is like a puzzle sentence. It is a rebus sentence where pictures represent some of the words in the sentence. Where are the rebus words in my sentence?

Students: A *fishy cracker* . . . *Goldfish is* one of those words!

Teacher: Yes, are there any other rebus words in my sentence?

Students: V8 juice

Teacher: Correct, are there any more?

Students: No!!

Teacher: Can you think of what we can add next to this message?

Student: We could write about our lunches.

Teacher: What shall we write then?

Student: I had Oreo cookies in my lunch.

Student: I brought a Yoplait™ yogurt in my lunchbox.

Assessment

Observe each student's active participation and ability to read the words.

Differentiation

- Place the message at a learning center and have the students read the message to each other independently.
- For a challenge, ask the students to write a complete story independently using environmental print as rebus words.

Rebus Writing with Environmental Print

Activity Format

Whole group

Objective

Students will read and write rebus sentences using environmental print in the place of some story words.

Materials

- a supply of environmental-print words
- glue
- paper
- chalkboard or whiteboard or chart paper
- scissors
- chalk or markers

Preparation

1. Prepare a set of familiar environmental-print words to use for the activity. Environmental print can be cut from newspaper ads, product packaging, and coupons, or printed from the computer. Multiple copies of some words may be needed if children choose the same word. For example, *McDonald's* is a popular, frequently chosen word for this activity.

2. Create one rebus sentence as an example for the class at the chalkboard or whiteboard, or on chart paper. For example, the rebus sentence might read, "We had Goldfish crackers and V8 fruit juice for our snack this morning." Product labels for *Goldfish* crackers and V8 juice should be in place of those words in the rebus sentence.

Procedure

1. Gather the students together. Show them the rebus sentence that you have created with the environmental-print words. Read it aloud once to the students.

2. Ask the students what they notice about the sentence. If necessary, say the environmental-print words slowly and draw their attention by pointing to each word of the sentence as you read. This tracking is important to connect each spoken word to the written word.

3. Tell the class that rebus sentences are like puzzles where pictures represent some of the words in the sentence. Ask them to identify the "puzzle" portion of your sample sentence.

4. Ask the students to reread your sample sentence with you aloud.

5. Have the children brainstorm ideas of what they would like to write in their own rebus sentences with partners.

6. Give them paper to write their sentences with the environmental-print words you have prepared for them.

7. Have the students read and reread their finished rebus sentences to other students.

Rebus Writing with Environmental Print (cont.)

Sample Dialog

Teacher: Boys and girls, look at this chart. I have written a special kind of message to you on it. Watch carefully as I read and point to the sentence.

Teacher reads the rebus sentence, using a pointer or a finger to show each word as it is read. "We had Ritz™ crackers and Juicy Juice for our snack this morning."

Teacher: What do you notice that is very different about this sentence that I have written?

Students: It has those picture words in it. You didn't write all the words yourself.

Teacher: Right! This is like a puzzle sentence. It is a rebus sentence, where pictures represent some of the words in the sentence. Where are the rebus words in my sentence?

Students: *Ritz* crackers. *Ritz* is one of those words!

Teacher: Yes. Are there any other rebus words in my sentence?

Students: *Juicy Juice.*

Teacher: Correct! Are there any more?

Students: No!

Teacher: Now it's your turn to write a rebus sentence like mine. I have all sorts of words for you to use in your sentence, and you may pick the ones you would like to use. Before you start to work, though, I want you to get into your share pairs and tell your partner exactly what your sentence is going to say. Then, you listen to your partner's sentence. Listen carefully, and tell your partner if you think the sentence is going to make good sense to all of us.

Assessment

Observe each student's ability to read the words. Observe the share-pair participation carefully. Assess the completed sentence for stages of writing development and fine motor control.

Differentiation

- Place the environmental-print words at a learning center and have the students repeat this activity independently.
- For a challenge, ask the students to write a complete story using environmental print rebus words.
- For a challenge, have the students try to combine their sentences with other students' sentences to create a story.

Echo Reading

Activity Format

Whole-group

Objective

Students will echo-read environmental-print writing to develop fluency, proper phrasing, and intonation.

Materials

- rebus sentences (See the lesson on pages 107–108.) or a pattern book with environmental print (See the lesson on pages 87–102.)
- overhead transparency film
- overhead marker

Preparation

1. Select a set of sentences or books from the previous lessons.
2. Make an overhead transparency of each sentence or book that you have selected.

Procedure

1. Gather students together. Display a sentence or first page of a book to the class.
2. Explain that you want the whole class to listen carefully to how you read the sentence.
3. Read the text aloud with careful enunciation, phrasing, and intonation for the class.
4. Use your finger or a pen to point to each word as you read it aloud. This tracking is important to connect spoken words to each written word.
5. Ask the class to reread the same text exactly as they heard you read it.
6. Repeat this activity again so that the students echo-read the same text twice.
7. Continue with the activity, reading through each overhead transparency.

Echo Reading (cont.)

Sample Dialog

Teacher: I have Johnny's rebus sentence on the overhead. I would like you to listen very carefully as I read what he wrote in his sentence. "I love McDonald's nuggets and Sonic™ Tater Tots." Now that I have read the sentence to you, I would like the whole class to echo-read the sentence with me, reading exactly the same way that I did. Emphasize the word *love* just as I did. Take a short breath after you say the word *and*. Let's try it together.

Students: "I love McDonald's nuggets and Sonic tater tots."

Teacher: Excellent. Let's try it again for extra good measure! "I love McDonald's nuggets and Sonic tater tots."

Students: "I love McDonald's nuggets and Sonic tater tots."

Teacher: You echo-read that very well. Great reading! Let's try another sentence.

Assessment

Observe for the students' active participation during the activity.

Differentiation

- Have groups of students echo-read.
- Challenge the students by having volunteer students lead the echo-reading.
- Students who struggle with this skill may need to echo-read more than twice. In small groups or with peer tutors, give these students more opportunities to echo-read.

Paired Reading

Activity Format

Small group

Objective

Students will participate in paired reading of environmental-print writing to develop fluency, proper phrasing, and intonation.

Materials

- rebus sentences (See the lesson on pages 107–108.) or a pattern book with environmental print (See the lesson on pages 87–102.)

Preparation

1. Select a set of sentences or books from a previous lesson.

Procedure

1. Gather students together into a small group.

2. Explain that you will demonstrate paired reading with a student. Ask the group to listen carefully as you read the sentence together.

3. Read the text aloud with the student partner, giving attention to enunciation, appropriate phrasing, and intonation for the class to hear. Use your finger or a pen to point to each word as you read it aloud together. This tracking is important to connect spoken words to each written word.

4. Ask the class to read their self-selected writing in pairs in the same way.

5. Repeat this activity again so that the students pair-read both sets of writing twice.

Paired Reading (cont.)

Sample Dialog

Teacher: Caroline and I are going to read her pattern book together in a very different way. Caroline and I are a pair, so we are calling this paired reading. Caroline will count to three and then we will begin reading together. We will read all the way through the pattern book, staying together as much as we can, sounding alike as much as we can. Are you ready, Caroline?

Caroline: One, two, three.

(Teacher and student read the pattern book through together.)

Teacher: Excellent reading, Caroline. Now, boys and girls, you are going to get into your pairs and you will pair-read the way that you heard Caroline and me reading.

Student: Which book should we read first?

Teacher: The partner who is younger will read his or her book first. So you need to compare your birthdates.

Assessment

Observe for the students' active participation during the activity.

Differentiation

- Challenge the students by having them pair-read longer books.
- Students who struggle with this skill may need more paired reading opportunities. Provide these students with more opportunities to echo-read with stronger readers.

Spin the Bottle Reading

Activity Format

Small group

Objective

Students will read and reread environmental-print words to develop word recognition and fluency.

Materials

- a supply of environmental-print words
- index cards
- chart paper or butcher paper
- markers
- empty plastic drink/water bottle
- scissors

Preparation

1. Prepare a set of environmental-print cards by gluing environmental-print words onto index cards. Environmental print can be cut from newspaper ads, product packaging, and coupons, or printed from the computer. Keep in mind that environmental print also consists of functional print, such as the name of your school, a stop sign, or an exit sign.

2. Laminate the environmental-print cards for durability, if desired.

3. Draw a large circle onto chart paper or onto butcher paper. The circle should be large enough for a group of children to gather around comfortably.

4. Divide the circle into six sections. You may also want to laminate the circle for durability.

Procedure

1. Gather the students together around the circle.

2. Sort the index cards into the six sections based on an attribute. For example, the words can be sorted by category, beginning letter, or number of syllables in the word.

3. Place the bottle in the center of the circle. Use the bottle as a spinner.

4. Show the students how to spin the bottle. Once the bottle has stopped spinning, the student at whom the bottle is pointing begins play. The student chooses a word from the section of the circle closest to his or her place on the circle, reads the word, spells the word, and then removes it from the circle.

5. Play continues in this manner until all the words have been removed from the circle.

Spin the Bottle Reading (cont.)

Sample Dialog

Teacher: Boys and girls, I have a set of cards made up with the words we have been collecting that we can read. I am going to divide the words into the sections of this circle by the type of word it is. I will put these into this section. Can you read the words aloud for me?

Students: *McDonald's, Burger King, Dairy Queen*™.

Teacher: Why do you think I put these words together?

Student: They are places you go to eat!

Teacher: Exactly! Now I am going to put these words into this section. Read these words with me.

Students: *On, Off, Exit, Entrance, Stop.*

Teacher: Why are these words all together?

Student: I know—they are all signs you read.

(The teacher continues placing cards into the circle.)

Teacher: Now that we have placed all of the cards into the circle, I am going to show you how to play the Spin the Bottle game. I will spin this bottle like this (spins bottle) and when it stops, the student it is pointing at begins the game.

Student: It stopped spinning on me!

Teacher: Yes it did. You choose a word from the section of the circle in front of you and read it aloud to us.

Student: Hmm…this one. *Arthur.*

Teacher: Now, spell the word for everyone to hear.

Student: **A-R-T-H-U-R**

Teacher: Excellent! Place the card out of the circle.

Assessment

Observe the students' participation as you sort the cards. Observe how well the students are able to spell the words.

Differentiation

- Place the game in a learning center so that the students can play the game independently.
- For greater difficulty, include words at differing levels of decontextualization, including manuscript versions of the same word.

"Go Fish" Reading

Activity Format

Small group with students in pairs/independent partner work

Objective

Students will match and read environmental-print words for encouraging word recognition and fluency.

Materials

- Functional-Print Cards (pages 36–39)
- a supply of environmental-print words
- glue
- index cards

Preparation

1. Prepare a set of environmental-print cards, with a minimum of five cards per student in the group. A particular word may be used four times per set of cards.
2. Duplicate four copies of the "Functional-Print Cards."
3. Glue each environmental-print word and functional-print word to an index card.
4. Laminate the cards for durability, if desired.

Procedure

1. Gather a small group of students. (This activity will first be done in a small group and then independently by students.)
2. Show students the cards and explain that they will be playing the Go Fish card game in pairs with the environmental-print words on the cards.
3. Model how the dealer passes out five cards to each student. Turn remaining cards facedown as a draw pile between each pair of students.
4. Begin play with the youngest student. The player should ask his or her partner for one matching environmental-print card. If the opponent holds the word, he or she gives it to the player and the player lays down the matched pair. If not, the opponent tells the player "Go fish," and the player picks up a card from the draw pile.
5. The opponent then continues play, asking for a word match. Play continues back and forth. The first student to lay all his or her cards down wins the game.
6. After having the children participate in this activity in a small group, encourage them to play independently for further practice.

"Go Fish" Reading (cont.)

Sample Dialog

Teacher: I have a deck of cards for each pair of you to play a game. To begin, I will be the dealer and I will give each of you five cards. Now you may look at your hand of cards and keep them to yourself. Only you will look at the cards. I will turn the rest of the deck over between the two of you and this will be the draw pile. The youngest student in your pair will start the game by asking the other player for a card that matches one of theirs.

Student: Ronnie, do you have a Taco Bell in your hand?

Student: No. Go fish!

Teacher: Alyssa, you take one card now from the draw deck.

Student: I drew a Taco Bell card!

Teacher: You got what you asked for; you may lay the pair of Taco Bell cards down now in front of you on the table. Ronnie, it is your turn to ask Alyssa for a card.

Student: Alyssa, do you have a STOP card?

Student: Yes! Here it is.

Teacher: Now, Ronnie, you have a pair of cards to lay down in front of you.

Assessment

Observe each student's ability to identify the words.

Differentiation

- For an added challenge, include decontextualized environmental-print words in manuscript print in the card deck.
- For an added challenge, include sight words in the card deck.
- Place the cards at a learning center. Have the students play the game independently.
- Card decks may go home as a family involvement activity.

Class Survey Book

Activity Format

Small group

Objective

Students will read environmental-print words and vote for favorites according to category to develop phonological knowledge and build vocabulary and comprehension skills. Results from the class survey will be published as a class-made book.

Materials

- "Graph Survey Sheets" (pages 119–122)
- a supply of environmental-print words
- crayons
- large sheets of cardstock paper
- scissors
- glue

Preparation

1. Create a graph on a sheet of cardstock paper. Headings for the graphs can include *Our Favorite Breakfast Food, Where Should We Go to Lunch?, Let's Go Shopping at . . .,* or I *Like to Play with. . . .*

2. Prepare a set of environmental-print words for use with this activity. Environmental print can be cut from newspaper ads, product packaging, and coupons, or printed from the computer. Keep in mind that environmental print also consists of functional print, such as the name of your school, a stop sign, or an exit sign. Multiple copies of some words may be needed if children choose the same words. For example, *McDonald's* is a popular, frequently chosen word for this activity.

Procedure

1. Direct the students to choose their favorite item in response to the graphing question.

2. Have the students glue the words onto the graph under the matching header to represent their choices for this survey question.

3. Discuss the graph results with the group of students. For example, ask the students "What does this graph show us? Which items does our group like the most? Which does our group like the least?"

4. Based on the discussion, ask the students to help you develop a caption for the graph.

5. Take the group responses as dictation and write this across the bottom of the graph page. This graph now becomes a page in a class survey book that showcases class preferences.

6. Have the students chorally read the dictated caption.

7. Create a cover for the Class Survey Book, and bind and place it in your classroom library for student reading and rereading.

Class Survey Book (cont.)

Sample Dialog

Teacher: I have made a special chart called a graph here. I would like to use it to find out what kinds of things you like the most. Today, I am going to ask, "What is your favorite breakfast food? I have three choices here. Do you see your favorite breakfast food?"

Student: I like Cheerios.

Teacher: Great! Do you see the word *Cheerios* there? Put some glue on it and put it on the graph. Does anyone else want to choose *Cheerios* as their favorite?

Student: I like Pop-Tarts™ the best. Can I put the word *Pop-Tarts* on the graph?

Teacher: Yes, you can put *Pop-Tarts* on the graph next to *Cheerios*.

Student: Not me! I love Krispy Kremes™. I want to put *Krispy Kremes* on the graph.

Teacher: All right, then, put *Krispy Kremes* on the graph beside *Pop-Tarts*. Now everyone else can glue their choice under yours.

Assessment

Observe the students' active participation and reading of the words. Use a class list as a checklist to note which words individual students have mastered.

Differentiation

- For an added challenge, have the students create and write each graph caption.
- Challenge the students by having them conduct a classroom poll on their own, with multiple copies of graphing pages.

Our Favorite Breakfast Food

#1	#2	#3

Where Should We Go to Lunch?

#1	#2	#3

I Like to Play with . . .

#1	#2	#3

Let's Go Shopping at . . .

#1	#2	#3

Stories in a Bag

Activity Format

Whole group

Objective

Students will tell a story using an environmental-print word in order to build an understanding of story structure.

Materials

- a supply of environmental-print words
- a bag
- scissors

Preparation

1. Prepare a set of familiar environmental-print words to use for the activity. Environmental print can be cut from newspaper ads, product packaging, and coupons, or printed from the computer. Keep in mind that environmental print also consists of functional print, such as the name of your school, a stop sign, or an exit sign.

2. Place the words in a bag.

Procedure

1. Direct a student to draw out one word from the bag.

2. Have the student read the word aloud.

3. Direct the student to think about his or her experiences with that word and then tell a story to the class from that real experience. For example, if a student draws *Wal-Mart* from the bag, the student might tell a story about his or her last visit to shop at Wal-Mart.

4. Storytelling helps children build a schema for a story and to develop story grammar. Listen for a beginning to the story, a series of events, and an outcome of the story as children tell their story. Probe their storytelling with questions to elicit more detail if necessary.

5. Continue the activity by having several other students select words from the storytelling bag.

Stories in a Bag (cont.)

Sample Dialog

Teacher:	This is my storytelling bag, and in this storytelling bag I have hidden some words that we are learning. I know that you can read these words very well. I am going to mix the words up completely. I would like to have a volunteer reach into my storytelling bag and draw out just one word. Who would like to be our first storyteller?
Student:	I would, I would!
Teacher:	All right, come up front and put your hand deep into the storytelling bag. Pick out just one of the words and read it to the whole class.
Student:	*Wal-Mart*! I picked out *Wal-Mart*.
Teacher:	Have you been to Wal-Mart?
Student:	Yes, I have.
Teacher:	Can you tell the whole class a story about going shopping at Wal-Mart?
Student:	My mom took me to Wal-Mart to go shopping for back to school. We bought a backpack, and scissors, and crayons, and glue.
Teacher:	Did you get any other school supplies at Wal-Mart?
Student:	We got some tissue for the class, too.
Teacher:	Did you get anything else while you were shopping at Wal-Mart?
Student:	Oh yeah, I got some new back-to-school clothes at Wal-Mart.
Teacher:	What else can you tell us about your shopping trip to Wal-Mart?
Student:	My mom and I ate a hot dog at Wal-Mart. I got to have some French fries with my hot dog, too. And then we went home with my new school supplies and my mom helped me put everything into my new backpack.

Assessment

Observe the students' active participation in the group. Use a class list as a checklist to note which students need further development of story structure and use of story grammar.

Differentiation

- Have the students pair up to tell stories to each other.
- Challenge the students to write their stories once they have finished the oral storytelling.
- Have the students choose multiple words to combine into one story.

Circular Storytelling with Environmental Print

Activity Format

Whole group

Objective

Students will tell a story using an environmental-print word in order to build an understanding of story structure.

Materials

- a supply of environmental-print words
- a bag
- scissors

Preparation

1. Prepare a set of environmental-print words to use for the activity. Environmental print can be cut from newspaper ads, product packaging, and coupons, or printed from the computer. Keep in mind that environmental print also consists of functional print, such as the name of your school, a stop sign, or an exit sign.
2. Place the environmental-print words in a bag.

Procedure

1. Direct a student to draw out one word from the bag.
2. Have the student read the word aloud.
3. Model for the students the beginning of this storytelling activity by starting the story line using the environmental-print word.
4. Storytelling helps children build a schema for story and to develop story grammar. Listen for a beginning to the story, a series of events, and an outcome of the story as children tell their story. Probe their storytelling with questions to elicit more detail if necessary.
5. Continue the activity by having one student at a time select a word from the storytelling bag and add onto the story with his or her word.

Circular Storytelling with Environmental Print (cont.)

Sample Dialog

Teacher: This is my storytelling bag, and in this storytelling bag I have hidden some words that we are learning. I know that you can read these words very well. I am going to mix the words up completely. I would like to have a volunteer reach into my storytelling bag and draw out just one word. Who would like to be our first storyteller?

Student: I would, I would!

Teacher: All right, come up front and put your hand deep into the storytelling bag. Pick out just one of the words and read it to the whole class.

Student: *Jack in the Box*. I picked out *Jack in the Box*.

Teacher: I am going to start our class circular story. Once I have begun the story, then each of you will choose a word to add on to the story. Let's start our story this way. "One afternoon, I was very hungry for a chicken cibatta sandwich from Jack in the Box." Now choose another word to keep our circular story going. Start with my sentence.

Student: I chose *Oreo*. "One afternoon I was very hungry for a chicken cibatta sandwich from Jack in the Box. I bought a package of Oreo cookies to eat with my chicken cibatta sandwich."

Teacher: Next, another student gets to choose a word and keep the story going.

Student: I chose EXIT. Do I use this now? "One afternoon I was very hungry for a chicken cibatta sandwich from Jack in the Box. I bought a package of Oreo cookies to eat with my Jack in the Box sandwich. I sat down near the exit to eat my lunch of Oreos and a Jack in the Box sandwich."

Assessment

Observe the students' active participation in the group. Use a class list as a checklist to note which students need further development of story structure and use of story grammar.

Differentiation

- Write the story as a language experience on chart paper. Place in a learning center for students to read and reread.
- Challenge the students to write the stories once you have finished the oral storytelling.
- Have the students take home the environmental-print words for writing a story with family members.

What's Going on Here? Critical Literacy with Environmental Print

Activity Format

Whole group

Objective

Students will examine and compare trademarks to critically infer advertisers' intent.

Materials

- a supply of familiar high-profile environmental-print words
- scissors

Preparation

1. Prepare a set of familiar, high-profile environmental-print words to use for the activity. Enlarging the environmental-print words for this activity will be very helpful so that all students can see the words clearly. Environmental print can be cut from newspaper ads, product packaging, and coupons, or printed from the computer. Keep in mind that environmental print also consists of functional print, such as the name of your school, a stop sign, or an exit sign.

2. Display the environmental-print words in front of the class so that all students can easily read them.

Procedure

1. Have the student read the environmental-print words aloud.

2. Ask the students what they notice about the set of words that you have displayed. Answers will vary and include a range of responses.

3. Guide the discussion to draw attention to the advertising intent of each company's trademark. For example, point out that the large capital **S** in *Safeway* is in the color red, and is designed to capture attention and stay in people's memory.

4. Continue the discussion examining the assortment of trademarks.

5. Ask the students to consider why the advertisers are trying to capture attention, remain in people's memory, etc. Ask the students to consider the goals advertisers have in designing trademarks for their products.

Fluency and Comprehension

What's Going on Here? Critical Literacy with Environmental Print (cont.)

Sample Dialog

Teacher: I have chosen some environmental-print words that we have been working with and that I know you can read very well. Let's start by reading through the words together.

(Students and teacher read through the displayed words.)

Teacher: Look very carefully at the words and tell me what you notice.

(Answers will vary and include a range of responses. Accept all answers from the students.)

Student: I notice that a lot of them are red letters.

Student: Look, the first letter is really big in all of the words.

Teacher: You are right. Why do you think the people who designed these trademarks for the companies wanted the letters to be big and red?

Student: Well, I think it is because they look nice.

Student: No, no, I think it is because you notice them right away.

Teacher: Do you just notice them?

Student: You can remember them easily, too. I have them in a picture in my mind.

Teacher: Why do think they want you to notice them and remember them?

Assessment

Observe the students' active participation in the group. Use a class list as a checklist to note which students are most perceptive about the intent of advertising signage.

Differentiation

- Have students expand the lesson by looking through newspaper and magazine ads with the same critical perspective.
- Challenge the students to design their own trademarks using their family names to capture attention.
- Have the students look through advertising materials at home with family members to critically discuss what advertisers are attempting to accomplish with product packaging.

3-D Environmental-Print Counting Book

Activity Format

Whole group

Objective

Students will create a class-made counting book.

Materials

- a supply of environmental-print words
- blank paper for book pages
- any counting book as a model (optional)
- scissors
- glue

Preparation

1. Prepare a set of familiar, high-profile environmental-print words to use for the activity. Environmental print can be cut from newspaper ads, product packaging, and coupons, or printed from the computer. Keep in mind that environmental print also consists of functional print, such as the name of your school, a stop sign, or an exit sign.

2. Gather the products for which you have environmental print. For example, if the word Cheerios is used, have a cup of Cheerios cereal available for the book.

Procedure

1. Read the counting book you have chosen as a model for this lesson to the class. Explain to the students that the class will be creating their very own counting book, using the environmental-print words that they have been reading and learning. Have the students read the words aloud.

2. Assign each student a number page for the book. Randomly pass out the words. Students will create their pages of the book based on the product and the number they have been assigned. For example, the student who is assigned the number six and Cheerios will glue six Cheerios onto the page and caption the page for the number six. Have the students glue the environmental-print word into the caption.

3. Direct students to complete the book page and to create an illustration of the caption with the real materials. Have students read their completed page to the whole class.

4. Bind the completed pages together. Create a cover for the class book. Place the completed book in the class library for students to read and reread.

3-D Environmental-Print Counting Book (cont.)

Sample Dialog

Teacher: I have chosen some environmental-print words that we have been working with and I know you can read very well. Let's start by reading through the words together.

(Students and teacher read through the words displayed together.)

Teacher: I have a page for our class counting book for each of you to complete. I have assigned each of you a number to create for the book. I am going to pass around the environmental-print words for you to use to create your number page.

Student: I have the number six.

Student: I have the number two.

Teacher: And you will use the M&M's label, and you will use the *Froot Loops* label.

Student: So I glue six M&M's onto my page?

Teacher: Yes. And what will you write under the M&M's as the caption for this page?

Student: Six M&M's. Do I glue the word M&M's here?

Teacher: Yes! You've got it!

Assessment

Observe the students' active participation in the activity. Evaluate each student's numeracy development and evaluate completed book page for stage of writing development and small motor control.

Differentiation

- Have the students expand the lesson by creating their own individual counting books.
- Challenge the students to create addition and subtraction sentences using environmental-print words and the real objects.
- Direct the students to take completed counting books home to read with family members.

What's Going on Here? Critical Literacy with Environmental Print #2

Activity Format

Small group

Objective

Students will examine and compare environmental print to critically infer advertisers' intent.

Materials

- a collection of magazines or newspaper advertisements
- scissors
- glue

Preparation

1. Gather students into small groups with a magazine or set of ads for each group.

Procedure

1. Ask the students to carefully go through the magazine and newspaper advertisements you have given them. Direct the group to cut out all of the product names for a specific category in the ads. For example, ask the students to cut out all of the words in food advertisements that they find. Direct another group to cut out all of the cleaning product names in their ads. Continue in this manner so that each group is searching for a different category of environmental-print words.

2. Have the students glue down the environmental-print words that they have found and cut out. Have students count the number of words they have located.

3. Ask the students to compare the results that they have found. Ask the students to determine who advertises the most. Who advertises the least? Is food most often advertised? Ask the students to consider what this might mean. Answers will vary and will include a range of responses.

4. Have the students create captions for their group pages. Bind the completed pages together. Create a cover for the class book. Place the completed book in the class library for students to read and reread.

What's Going on Here? Critical Literacy with Environmental Print #2 (cont.)

Sample Dialog

Teacher: I have brought a group of magazines for you to work with today. I would like you to work in your table groups with one magazine. Each table group will look carefully for ads for the products that I have assigned to you.

(Students and teacher read through the assigned products together.)

Teacher: I have a page for our book for each group to complete. I would like you to cut out every advertisement for food (stores, cleaning products, etc.) that you find in your magazine and glue it down to the page.

Student: We have stores. I just found a page for Target™.

Student: And here is a page for Wal-Mart.

Teacher: Excellent! Cut out the store names from those advertisements and glue them to your page.

Student: We have food. Do vitamins count as food?

Teacher: Yes, let's include vitamins on our food page. Now, when you are done, go back and count how many names you have glued down on your pages.

Assessment

Observe the students' active participation in the group. Evaluate each student's numeracy development and evaluate the completed book pages for stage of writing development and fine-motor control.

Differentiation

- Have the students expand the lesson by creating their own individual books.
- Challenge the students with a discussion of the dangers of eating too much sugar, using unsafe products, etc. Write letters to the manufacturer expressing concern for the impact their product might have.
- Direct the students to take their completed books home to read and reread with family members.

Building Vocabulary

Opportunities abound within the typical classroom for children to learn new vocabulary and to experiment with words. To learn new words, children must experience words in frequent, meaningful, and varied contexts. The more exposure a child has to words, the better able he or she is to read and comprehend. Vocabulary knowledge, then, is an important factor in reading comprehension.

Sight words are those high-frequency words that do not necessarily decode and that must be read with automaticity by children. The lessons in this section provide oral-reading opportunities to children of varying reading levels and different learning styles in a whole-class setting or in a small-group setting. The lessons and activities reinforce the sight words that children must recognize automatically. Sight words are repeated to develop visual memory and improve visual-auditory perception.

Vocabulary learning is comprised of roughly four stages: listening, speaking, reading, and writing. Children develop these components of vocabulary in this sequence as well. A child's first vocabulary is the listening vocabulary. He or she arrives at school with a receptive vocabulary of thousands and thousands of words. Speaking vocabulary develops after the listening vocabulary. Reading and writing vocabulary begin expanding dramatically after the age of five or six. For very young children, the first words learned are those that are experienced within the home, family, and caregiving environments. As children interact with their environment, they construct and learn concepts for which words become labels. The environment for young children includes experiences with words on products, packaging, signs, and billboards.

Following basic principles for developing vocabulary with young children, the subsequent lesson plans use environmental print to:

- Teach useful words that young children will likely encounter.
- Teach words that are conceptually related to others.
- Teach words that relate to their background knowledge.
- Generate an enthusiasm for and interest in words.

Environmental-Print Word Sort

Activity Format

Small group

Objective

Students will do an **open sort** of environmental-print words to develop word recognition, build vocabulary, and develop categorization skills.

Materials

- a supply of environmental-print words
- scissors

Preparation

1. Prepare a set of environmental-print words to use for the activity. Environmental print can be cut from newspaper ads, product packaging, and coupons, or printed from the computer. Keep in mind that environmental print also consists of functional print, such as the name of your school, a stop sign, or an exit sign.

Procedure

1. Gather the students together. Show the students the environmental-print words that you have prepared.
2. Ask students which words could be grouped together.
3. Read aloud through the environmental-print words with the group. Encourage students to look for shared features in the words.
4. Consider all possibilities as the students offer ways to group and regroup the words together. Some grouping possibilities might include types of product or business represented, type of font used, beginning letter of the word, and color or size of the word.
5. Continue this activity, combining the sorted groups back again and resorting in a different manner.

Environmental-Print Word Sort (cont.)

Sample Dialog

Teacher: I have some words that you know how to read and I would like to read them out loud with you.

(Students and teacher read through the set of environmental-print words together.)

Teacher: Can you think of a way that we could sort these words into groups?

Student: We could sort these words into groups of things you eat, and everything else.

Teacher: All right, good! Let's sort these into two groups. One group will be things you can eat and the other group will be everything else.

(Students and teacher separate the environmental-print words into two groups.)

Teacher: Let's read through all the words that we have in our group of things you can eat! Listen carefully and be certain that we have sorted correctly. Only words for things that we eat belong in this group. Then, let's read through all the words that we have in the group of everything else.

(Students and teacher read through the groups of environmental-print words together.)

Teacher: Now I am going to mix the words back together and we'll try to think of a different way to sort these words.

Assessment

Observe the students' participation during this activity. Using a class list as a checklist, note the words the students are able to instantly recognize and read.

Differentiation

- Conduct the same activity, challenging the students to sort the words into three or more groups at a time.
- Place the environmental-print words in a learning center with specific categories for the students to sort.
- Conduct the same activity using other new vocabulary words, student names, and sight words.
- Send the words home with the students to sort with family members. Challenge the students to add new words to the group with family members.

Building Vocabulary

Environmental–Print Word Sort with a Venn Diagram

Activity Format

Small group

Objective

Students will do a closed sort of environmental-print words to develop word recognition, build vocabulary, and develop categorization skills.

Materials

- "Venn Diagram Template" (page 138)
- a supply of environmental-print words
- scissors

Preparation

1. Prepare a set of environmental-print words to use for the activity. Environmental print can be cut from newspaper ads, product packaging, and coupons, or printed from the computer. Keep in mind that environmental print also consists of functional print, such as the name of your school, a stop sign, or an exit sign.

2. Photocopy the "Venn Diagram Template." Determine which two categories we use to label the diagram. For example, grocery stores and "other." Alternately, the categories may use characteristics of the environmental print, such as words that are all capital letters and words that are all lowercase letters.

Procedure

1. Gather the students together. Show the students the environmental-print words that you have prepared. Read through the words aloud with the whole group.

2. Show the students the Venn diagram. Explain to the students that the diagram will help them sort the words.

3. Ask the students which words can be grouped together in each of the two categories.

4. Encourage the students to look for shared features in the two groups of words to make up the common category of the Venn diagram.

5. Take all possibilities as the students offer ways to group and regroup the words together.

Environmental-Print Sort with a Venn Diagram (cont.)

Sample Dialog

Teacher: I have some words that you know how to read, and I would like to read them aloud with you.

(Students and teacher read through the set of environmental-print words together.)

Teacher: I have our Venn diagram ready to help us sort these words into two different groups. One side of the Venn diagram is words that use only capital letters. Can you look through the words we have and find the words that are just capital letters?

Student: Here is PEPSI. It is all in capital letters.

Student: BAND-AID is all in capital letters, too.

Student: BURGER KING is also in capitals.

Student: And ELMO™ writes his name in all uppercase letters.

(Students and teacher sort and separate the words.)

Teacher: All right, good! The other side of the Venn diagram is for words that use only lowercase letters. Can you look through the words that are left and find the ones that are written in lowercase letters?

Student: fry's™ is all in lowercase.

Student: ups™

(Students and teacher sort and separate the words.)

Teacher: Let's read all the words we have in our two groups. Look carefully at each word and to be certain that we have sorted correctly.

Assessment

Observe the students' participation during this activity. Using a class list as a checklist, note the words students are able to instantly recognize and read.

Differentiation

- Conduct the same activity, challenging the students to sort the words into three, four, or more groups.
- Place the environmental-print words in a learning center for the students to sort.
- Conduct the same activity using other new vocabulary words, student names, and sight words.
- Send the words home with the student to sort with family members. Challenge the students to add new words to the group with family members.

Venn Diagram

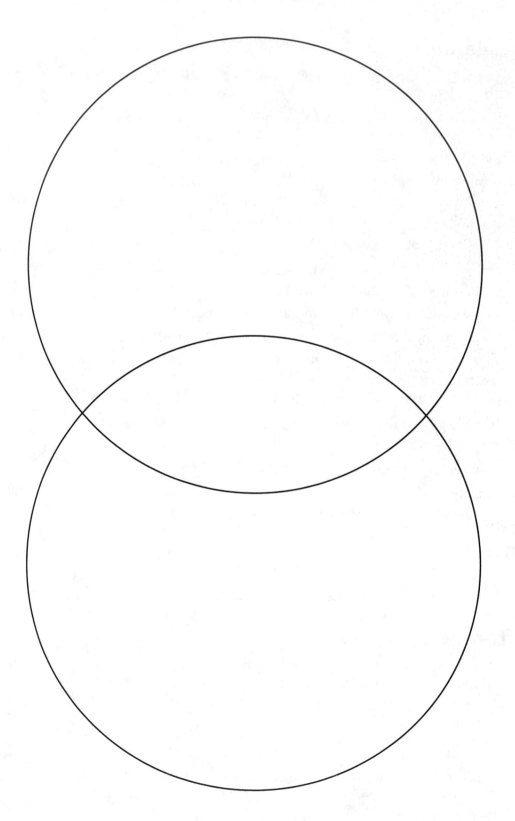

Word Mapping with Environmental Print

Activity Format

Small group

Objective

Students will learn simple word mapping using familiar environmental-print words.

Materials

- a supply of environmental-print words
- chalkboard or whiteboard or chart paper
- markers
- scissors

Preparation

1. Prepare a set of environmental-print words to use for the activity. Environmental print can be cut from newspaper ads, product packaging, and coupons, or printed from the computer. Keep in mind that environmental print also consists of functional print, such as the name of your school, a stop sign, or an exit sign.

Procedure

1. Gather students together into a small group. Show them the set of familiar environmental-print words that you have gathered for the activity.
2. Ask the students to help you select an environmental-print word that the group will use together.
3. Place the word in the middle of a chalkboard, whiteboard, or chart paper.
4. Draw a box around the word to begin developing the word map.
5. Ask the students to use their five senses to describe the word. "What is it?" "What is it like?" "What are some examples?"
6. Write these on the chalkboard, whiteboard, or chart paper as the students offer them. Develop the word map from these words. Have students read through all the words with you.

Word Mapping with Environmental Print (cont.)

Sample Dialog

Teacher: Boys and girls, I have some words here that I know are very familiar to you. I know that you can read these words well. We have used them in a lot of other ways. What one word should we choose to work with today?

Student: *Cheerios.*

Teacher: I am going to put the word *Cheerios* on the chart paper and draw a square around it. What are Cheerios?

Students: Cereal.

Students: We eat it for breakfast.

Students: They are round circles of oats.

Teacher: Good. Good. Wait just a moment for me to write down all the words that you are saying to me.

(Teacher writes down the words the students offer to define *Cheerios*.)

Teacher: We have cereal, food for breakfast, and round oat circles. Now tell me what Cheerios are like.

Students: Crunchy.

Students: They float in milk.

Assessment

Observe the students' participation in the group. Use a class list as a checklist to note which students participate. If necessary, take extra time to emphasize the words used to develop the word map.

Differentiation

- Place the materials at a learning center and encourage the students to continue expanding the map with more descriptors.
- Place the materials at a learning center and encourage the students to repeat the activity independently with other environmental-print words.
- Read and reread the words in varying groups and patterns. For example, boys and girls alternate reading; read slowly; read quickly; read softly; read loudly.

Cherrios Word Map

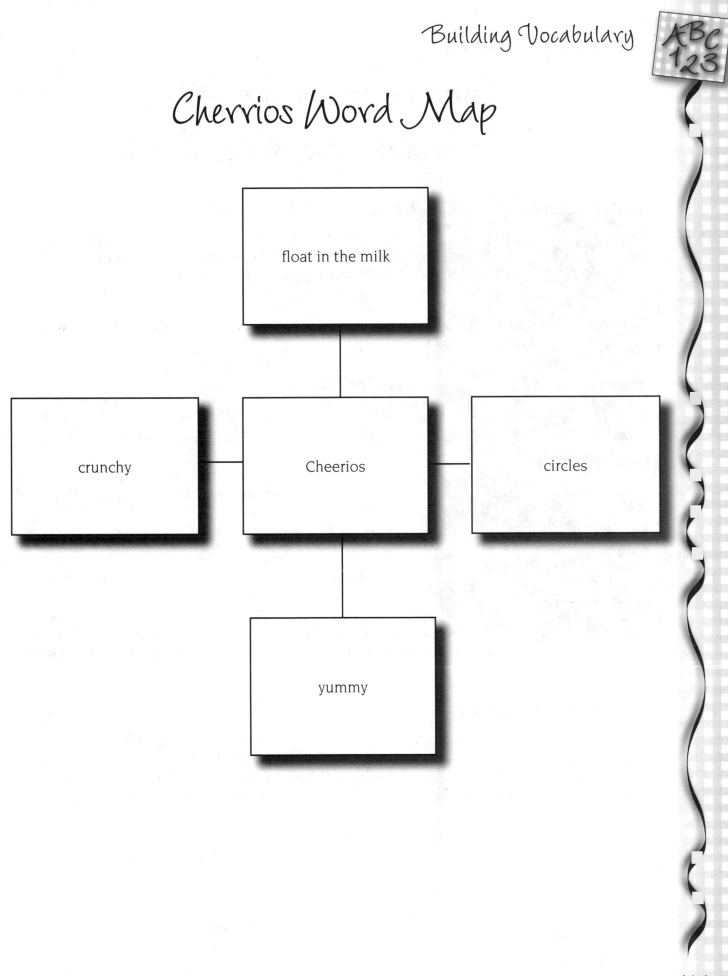

float in the milk

crunchy — Cheerios — circles

yummy

Mapping Experiences with Environmental-Print Words

Activity Format

Small group

Objective

Students will learn simple experience mapping using familiar environmental-print words.

Materials

- a supply of environmental-print words
- chalkboard or whiteboard or chart paper
- markers
- scissors

Preparation

1. Prepare a set of environmental-print words to use for the activity. Environmental print can be cut from newspaper ads, product packaging, and coupons, or printed from the computer. Keep in mind that environmental print also consists of functional print, such as the name of your school, a stop sign, or an exit sign.

Procedure

1. Gather students together into a small group. Show them the set of environmental print that you have gathered for the activity.

2. Ask the students to help you select an environmental-print word that the group will use together.

3. Place the word in the middle of a chalkboard, whiteboard, or chart paper.

4. Draw a box around the word to begin developing the semantic web.

5. Ask the students to describe their experiences with the word makes them think of. For example, if the word is *McDonald's*™, the students may offer French fries, Ronald McDonald, hamburgers, and Happy Meal™.

6. Write these on the chalkboard, whiteboard, or chart paper as the students offer them. Develop the semantic map from these words. Have students read through all the words with you.

Mapping Experiences with Environmental-Print Words (cont.)

Sample Dialog

Teacher: Boys and girls, I have a set of words here that I know are very familiar to you. I know that you can read these words well. We have used them in a lot of other ways. What one word should we choose to work with today?

Students: McDonald's . . . yeah, McDonald's.

Teacher: I am going to put McDonald's on the chart paper and draw a box around it. Think about the last time you went to McDonalds. What things do you think about when we say McDonald's?

Students: Hamburgers.

Students: Ronald McDonald.

Students: Playland™.

Teacher: Good. Good. Wait just a moment for me to write down all the words that you are saying to me.

(Teacher writes down the words associated with McDonald's on the chart.)

Teacher: We have *hamburgers* here, *Ronald McDonald* here, and *Playland*. Well, what other words do you think of when you think of McDonald's?

Students: French fries.

Students: Happy Meals.

Assessment

Observe students participation in the group. Use a class list as a checklist to note which students participate. If necessary, take extra time to emphasize the words used to develop the experience map.

Differentiation

- Place the materials at a learning center and encourage the students to continue expanding the map with more descriptors.
- Place the materials at a learning center and encourage the students to repeat the activity independently with other environmental-print words.
- Read and reread the descriptor words in varying groups and patterns. For example, boys and girls alternate reading; read slowly; read quickly; read softly; read loudly.

Sample Experience Map for McDonald's

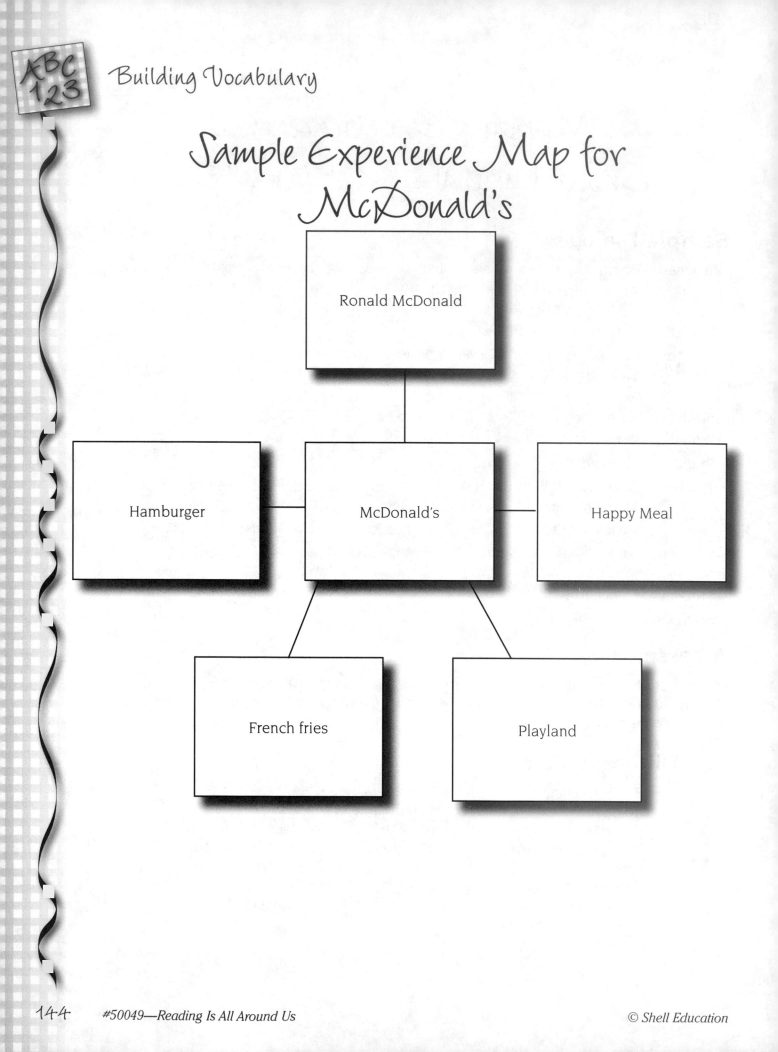

Ronald McDonald

Hamburger — McDonald's — Happy Meal

French fries

Playland

My Very Own Word Bank

Activity Format

Small group

Objective

Students will practice vocabulary words to expand sight-reading vocabulary and increase automaticity.

Materials

- "My Very Own Word Bank" (page 147)
- a supply of environmental-print words
- cardstock weight paper
- scissors

Preparation

1. Prepare a set of environmental-print words to use for the activity. Environmental print can be cut from newspaper ads, product packaging, and coupons, or printed from the computer. Keep in mind that environmental print also consists of functional print, such as the name of your school, a stop sign, or an exit sign.

2. Photocopy the template for "My Very Own Word Bank" onto cardstock for durability. Prepare one copy per student.

Procedure

1. Begin by explaining to the students that vocabulary words are words that they should be able to read quickly. Show them the set of familiar environmental-print words that you have prepared.

2. Have the students read through the set of environmental-print words with you aloud.

3. Listen to each student read the environmental-print words independently. Note which words are the most challenging for each student. For each student, select six words, including some challenging words, to begin the student's word bank.

4. Give students directions for copying the environmental-print words onto their "My Very Own Word Bank" cards. Cut along the dotted lines.

5. Have students practice reading the words from their word bank cards. Have students trade cards and practice with a fellow student to increase confidence and automatic reading.

6. The cards can be put onto rings, put into zipper plastic bags, or stored in file card boxes for each child to use during language activities.

My Very Own Word Bank (cont.)

Sample Dialog

Teacher: Boys and girls, I have a set of words here that I know are very familiar to you. I know you can read these words well. We have used them in a lot of other ways. I want to read through all of these words with you aloud today.

(Teacher and students read through all of the words in the set of prepared environmental-print words.)

Teacher: Now, I would like you to write these six words to create cards for your Very Own Word Bank. Your job right now is to write those words down onto your blank card sheet. Put one word into each card. When you are done, cut along the dotted lines and you will have six new cards for your word bank.

(Students copy the environmental-print words onto the card template.)

Student: I finished my cards!

Teacher: Now you can begin to use your Word Bank cards by quietly reading them.

Assessment

Observe the students' participation in the group. Use a class list as a checklist to note which words the students are struggling to read.

Differentiation

- Place the materials at a learning center and encourage the students to continue the activity independently with other words.
- Read and reread the words in varying groups and patterns. For example, boys and girls alternate reading; read slowly; read quickly; read softly; read loudly.
- Have the students take their word bank cards home to read with a family member as a family involvement activity.

My Very Own Word Bank

Building Vocabulary

Teaching Simple Analogies with Environmental Print

Preparation

1. Prepare a set of environmental-print words to use for the activity. Environmental print can be cut from newspaper ads, product packaging, and coupons, or printed from the computer. Keep in mind that environmental print also consists of functional print, such as the name of your school, a stop sign, or an exit sign.

Procedure

1. Show the students the set of familiar environmental-print words that you have prepared.
2. Have the students read through the words with you aloud.
3. Choose two words that are related and ask the students to explain the relationship between the two. For example, choose the words *Safeway* and *fry's*.
4. Student explanations may vary, but arrive at the relationship that both are grocery stores.
5. Continue the analogy by adding a second relationship to the analogy. For example, *Safeway* is to *fry's* as *Burger King* is to_____. Ask the students to explain what might fit into the blank. Student explanations may vary but arrive at the relationship that *Safeway* and *fry's* are grocery stores, *Burger King* and *McDonald's*, *Taco Bell*, *Sonic*, etc. are fast-food restaurants.
6. Continue building analogies using the environmental print as manipulatives to create these analogies.

Teaching Simple Analogies with Environmental Print (cont.)

Sample Dialog

Teacher: Boys and girls, I have a set of words here that I know are very familiar to you. I know you can read these words well. We have used them in a lot of other ways. I want to read through all of these words with you aloud today.

(Teacher and students read through all of the words in the set of prepared environmental-print words.)

Teacher: Now, I am taking two of the words out of this group. How are these two words related? How are they alike?

Student: *Safeway* and *fry's* are both grocery stores.

Teacher: Yes, they are. So, *Safeway* is related to *fry's* because they are both grocery stores. Now I am going to add two more words. But one of them is secret. The new words will be related to each other in the same way that *Safeway* is related to *fry's*.

Student: That one is *Burger King*.

Teacher: Yes, so what could be like *Burger King* the way that *Safeway* is like *fry's*?

Student: Is it *McDonald's*?

Teacher: It could be. How is *Safeway* to *fry's* the same way that *Burger King* is to *McDonald's*?

Student: They are both hamburger restaurants.

Assessment

Observe the students' participation in the group. Use a class list as a checklist to note which the students grasp the analogies you create.

Differentiation

- Place the materials at a learning center and encourage the students to repeat the activity independently with other environmental print.
- Challenge the students to create their own analogies.
- Challenge the students to write out the analogies using the notation of **:** and **::** to signify an analogy. For example, Safeway: grocery store :: McDonalds: restaurant.

Building Vocabulary

Word Sorting with Body Percussion

Activity Format

Whole group

Objective

Students will sort environmental-print words based on the rhythmic pattern of body percussion arrangements.

Materials

- a supply of environmental-print words
- scissors

Preparation

1. Prepare a set of environmental-print words to use for the activity. Environmental print can be cut from newspaper ads, product packaging, and coupons, or printed from the computer. Keep in mind that environmental print also consists of functional print, such as the name of your school, a stop sign, or an exit sign.

2. Place the environmental-print words on the board for students to see or use the Environmental-Print Word Wall (see pages 67–68).

Procedure

1. Direct the students' attention to the familiar environmental-print words that you have prepared.

2. Have the students read through the words with you out loud.

3. Review with the students how to create a rhythm using body percussion. Begin by snap-clapping an AB pattern. Once the whole class has the snap-clap pattern synchronized, ask them to call out words that fit the pattern. For example, LEGO, *Arby's*, *Band-Aid*, *Goldfish*, and *KitKat* are all two-syllable words that would fit the AB pattern.

4. Separate these words out into one group.

5. Continue the activity by changing the body percussion rhythm to an ABC pattern such as snap-clap-slap thigh. Once the whole class has the snap-clap-slap thigh pattern synchronized, ask them to call out words that fit this pattern. (For example, *Apple Jacks*, *Burger King*, *Cheerios*, *Lucky Charms*™, *Pizza Hut*.)

6. Separate these words out into another group.

7. Continue the activity by changing the body percussion rhythm to an ABCD pattern such as snap-clap-slap thigh-tap head. Once the whole class has the snap-clap-slap thigh-tap head pattern synchronized, ask them to call out words with this pattern. (For example, *Peter Piper*™, *Jelly Belly*, *Coca Cola*™.)

8. Separate these words into another group.

9. Explain to the students that you have just sorted the words by the number of syllables in each word.

Word Sorting with Body Percussion (cont.)

Sample Dialog

Teacher: Boys and girls, I have a set of words here that I know are very familiar to you. I know that you can read these words well. We have used them in a lot of other ways. I want to read through all of these words with you out loud today.

(Teacher and students read through all of the words.)

Teacher: Now, I am going to begin a snap-clap pattern and I want you to join in.

(Teacher and students snap-clap in unison.)

Teacher: What words are on the board that fit this pattern? I will start. Ar-by's, Ar-by's, Ar-by's, Ar-by's. Can you hear the AB pattern as we continue snap-clapping? Now you try. What words on the board are the same pattern?

(Teacher and students snap-clap in unison. Students call out their guesses to fit the body percussion pattern.)

Assessment

Observe the students' active participation in the group. Use a class list as a checklist to note which students can discern the syllables within each word.

Differentiation

- Place the environmental-print words at a learning center and encourage the students to repeat the activity independently using manipulatives to create the pattern.
- Challenge the students to create their own body percussion rhythms.

Building Vocabulary

Compound Words in Environmental Print

Preparation

1. Prepare a set of environmental-print words to use for the activity. Environmental print can be cut from newspaper ads, product packaging, and coupons, or printed from the computer. Keep in mind that environmental print also consists of functional print, such as the name of your school, a stop sign, or an exit sign.

Procedure

1. Direct the students' attention to the familiar environmental-print words that you have prepared.
2. Have the students read through the set of words with you aloud.
3. Explain to the students that a compound word is a word made of two other words. Sometimes the new word is like the two smaller words but sometimes it is completely different and means something completely different than the two smaller words.
4. Find a compound word in the set of words that you have prepared. For example, *Goldfish* is a compound word that does not necessarily mean *gold* (a precious metal) and *fish* (aquatic life) when referring to small snack crackers.
5. Continue the activity by having students look for compound words. Discuss with the students whether the word means what it says.

Compound Words in Environmental Print (cont.)

Sample Dialog

Teacher: Boys and girls, I have a set of words here that I know are very familiar to you. I know that you can read these words well. We have used them in a lot of other ways. I want to read through all of these words with you out loud today.

(Teacher and students read through all of the words in the set of prepared environmental-print words.)

Teacher: This word is in our set of words. *Goldfish*. What two words do think make up this word?

Student: *Gold* and *fish*!

Teacher: Yes! *Gold* and *fish* are put together to make up a new word *Goldfish*. We call the new word a compound word. Look through the rest of the words with me and tell me if you see any other words like this that are made up of two other words.

(Teacher and students read through all of the words in the set of words. Students will offer unexpected responses and each should be accepted as good thinking but be certain to focus on the two words in a compound word.)

Assessment

Observe the students' active participation in the group. Use a class list as a checklist to note which students can discern the components of a compound word.

Differentiation

- Place the environmental-print words at a learning center and encourage the students to repeat the activity independently, using manipulatives to create the pattern.
- Challenge the students to find other compound words in literature, student dictionaries, etc.

Building Vocabulary

Sketch to Stretch for Compound Words

Activity Format

Small group

Objective

Students will draw compound words from environmental print.

Materials

- a supply of environmental-print words, some of which are compound words
- drawing paper
- markers, crayons, or colored pencils
- scissors

Preparation

1. Prepare a set of familiar environmental-print words, some of which are compound words, to use for the activity. Environmental print can be cut from newspaper ads, product packaging, and coupons, or printed from the computer. Keep in mind that environmental print also consists of functional print, such as the name of your school, a stop sign, or an exit sign.

2. Fold the drawing paper in trifold fashion, right edge folded to the paper center and left edge to the paper center.

Procedure

1. Direct the students' attention to the familiar environmental-print words that you have prepared.

2. Have the students read through the set of words with you aloud.

3. Explain to the students that a compound word is a word made of the two other words. Sometimes the new word is like the two smaller words, but sometimes it is completely different and means something different than the two smaller words.

4. Find a compound word in the set of words that you have prepared. For example, *Goldfish* is a compound word that does not necessarily mean *gold* (a precious metal) and *fish* (aquatic life) when referring to small snack crackers.

5. Continue the activity by having students look for compound words. Discuss with the students whether the word means what it says.

6. Have the students glue the compound word inside the folded paper. Close the right and left flaps over the environmental-print word(s). On the left side flap, write the first word in the compound word. On the right side flap, write the second word of the compound word. Have the students draw and color an illustration for each part of the compound word. When the paper is opened, the environmental print version of the compound word appears.

Sketch to Stretch for Compound Words (cont.)

Sample Dialog

Teacher: Boys and girls, I have a set of words here that I know are very familiar to you. I know you can read these words well. We have used them in a lot of other ways. I want to read through all of these words with you out loud today.

(Teacher and students read through all of the words in the set of prepared environmental-print words.)

Teacher: This word is in our set of words: *Goldfish*. What two words do you think make up this word?

Student: *Gold* and *fish*!

Teacher: Yes! *Gold* and *fish* are put together to make up a new word *Goldfish*. We call the new word a compound word. Look through the rest of the words with me and tell me if you see any other words like this that are made up of two other words.

(Teacher and students read through all of the words in the set of environmental-print words. Students will offer unexpected responses and each should be accepted as good thinking, but be certain to focus on the two words in a compound word.)

Teacher: Now that we have found the compound words, I want you to choose an environmental-print compound word and glue it inside the cover of the folded sheet of paper. Then, close your paper and write the two words that make up the compound word on the front. Write the first part of the word on the left side of the folded paper. Write the second part of the word on the right side of the paper. When you have finished writing in the two parts that make up this compound word, illustrate each part of the word.

Student: I have *Blockbuster*™. My two words are *block* and *buster*. How should I illustrate the *buster* part of the word?

Assessment

Observe the students' active participation in the group. Use a class list as a checklist to note which students can discern the components of a compound word. Also, you may note which students can distinguish whether there is a logical connection between the two words that make up the compound word. Evaluate the completed illustrations.

Differentiation

- Place the environmental-print words at a learning center and encourage students to repeat the activity independently.
- Challenge the students to find other compound words in literature,

Decontextualized Vocabulary Collage

Activity Format

Small group

Objective

The student will identify common words in environmental-print words.

Materials

- a supply of environmental-print words
- scissors
- glue
- construction paper

Preparation

1. Prepare a set of environmental-print words. Each should contain a common word that is familiar to the children. For example, *Pizza Hut* contains the word *pizza*. A stop sign contains the word *stop*. See the examples below:

   > Apple Jacks (*apple*)
   >
   > Hershey's Crunch™ (*crunch*)
   >
   > Kit Kat (*kit*)
   >
   > Jack in the Box (*in, the, box*)
   >
   > IN-N-OUT Burger™ (*in and out*)
   >
   > Hello Kitty™ (*hello, kitty*)
   >
   > Tootsie Roll (*roll*)
   >
   > Sesame Street (*street*)
   >
   > Pizza Hut (*pizza*)
   >
   > Play-Doh (*play*)

Procedure

1. Review the names of the featured environmental-print words. Ask students to tell how they know the name of each. Were there letters they recognized? Were there graphics they recognized?

2. Explain that many environmental-print words contain common words that we use all the time. For example, display the word *Play-Doh* and have the students read it.

3. Ask the students to identify the word that is commonly used (*play*).

4. Cut out the word *play* and glue only that portion of the product name to the construction paper.

5. Continue in this manner with the remaining words; then review each of the common words glued to the construction paper.

Decontextualized Vocabulary Collage (cont.)

Sample Dialog

Teacher: Many environmental-print words have words we use every day. Look at this word *Play-Doh*. What does it say?

Student: *Play-Doh*!

Teacher: Is there a word in *Play-Doh* that we use often?

Student: *Play*!

Teacher: That's right! The word *play* is in *Play-Doh*. So, if you can read *Play-Doh*, you can read *play*. (Teacher cuts out the word *play* and glues it to the construction paper.) Let's read this word together.

Student: *Play*.

Assessment

Observe as the students participate in the activity. Check for students' understanding that common words are often found in environmental-print words.

Differentiation

- For a challenge, have the students write the common words on paper so they can see how the words look when written in pencil.
- Encourage the students to locate other environmental-print words that contain common words. Invite them to bring in product packaging and coupons, or newspaper ads from home that contain these words.

Building Vocabulary

Vocabulary Bingo

Activity Format

Small group

Objective

Students will identify common words in environmental-print words.

Materials

- "Bingo Card" (page 160)
- a supply of environmental-print words
- scissors
- marker
- game markers (such as beans or buttons)

Preparation

1. Locate environmental-print words that contain common words familiar to the children. For example, *Sesame Street* contains the word *street*. IN-N-OUT B*urger* contains the words *in* and *out*.

2. Duplicate the "Bingo Card" for each student in the group. On each square of the "Bingo Card," write a common word, using a marker. Write words such as *kit, street, play, box, hello*. Be sure that each bingo cards has words written in random order and that you have an environmental-print word containing each common word on the cards.

3. Gather markers such as beans or buttons.

Procedure

1. Provide each child with a bingo card and nine game markers.

2. Select an environmental-print word and show it to the students. Ask the students to say the word(s) and identify a common word in it.

3. Instruct the students to locate this word on their Bingo cards. Tell them that the word will not have the graphics or colors that are shown in the environmental print.

4. Each student who finds this word on his or her card covers it with a game marker.

5. A student who covers four squares in a row (horizontally, diagonally, or vertically) wins that round of play.

Vocabulary Bingo (cont.)

Sample Dialog

Teacher:	(Teacher displays the words *Sesame Street*.) What does this say?
Student:	*Sesame Street!*
Teacher:	Let's look carefully at these words. Is there a common word you know in *Sesame Street*?
Student:	*Street*.
Teacher:	Yes, the second word says *street*. Find *street* on your bingo card and, if you have it, cover it with a bingo marker. Who can use the word *street* in a sentence?
Student:	I live right down the *street*.
Student:	What *street* do you live on?
Student:	My house is on Maple *Street*.

Assessment

Observe the students as they participate in the activity. Check for their understanding that common words are often found in environmental-print words. Pay close attention as they attempt to use the words in sentences and as they identify decontextualized words on their Bingo cards.

Differentiation

- Create bingo cards with other common words and have the students play independently or in small groups at a learning center.
- Challenge the students to use decontextualized words from environmental print in their writing.

Bingo Card

B	I	N	G	O

Find the Common Word

Activity Format

Small group

Objective

Students will identify common words in environmental-print words.

Materials

- a supply of environmental-print words
- pencils
- writing paper
- scissors

Preparation

1. Locate environmental-print words that contain common words familiar to the children. For example, *Apple Jacks* contains the word *apple*. *Jack in the Box* contains the words *in*, *the*, and *box*.

2. Cut out the environmental-print words and laminate them for durability, if desired.

Procedure

1. Gather a small group of students at a table.

2. Remind students of the previous lesson where they located common words contained in environmental-print words.

3. Ask the students what they remember from the lesson and the common words they were able to find.

4. Tell the students that they will do the same kind of activity in this lesson, but they will have the opportunity to write the words they find.

5. Distribute paper and pencils to the students. Then, hold up an environmental-print word, such as *Jack in the Box*. Ask the students to read the word.

6. Next, ask the students to determine which words in *Jack in the Box* are common words we use just about every day. (Students will likely identify *in*, *the*, and possibly *box*.)

7. Instruct each child to write each word on a separate line of the paper. Point out that the words look different now. In the environmental print, the words are large, fat, and white. They look very different from the words written in pencil, but the letters are still shaped basically the same.

8. Ask students to think of sentences that include one or all of these words.

Find the Common Word (cont.)

Sample Dialog

Teacher: (Teacher holds up *Jack in the* Box.) What does this say?

Student: *Jack in the* Box!

Teacher: Say it again and try to figure out which words in *Jack in the* Box are common words that we use every day.

Student: *In* and *the* are common words.

Teacher: That's right! Write the word *in* on the first line of your paper. Then, write the word *the* below it. Do these words look the same as they do on the sample?

Student: No, the words in the sample are white and tilted to the side.

Teacher: That's right. Who can use one or both of these words in a sentence?

Student: My cat got *in the* drawer.

Assessment

Review the students' writing of common words and pay attention to their participation in the group activity.

Differentiation

- Challenge the students to write complete sentences using the common words they find.
- Encourage the students to locate other environmental-print words that contain common words. Invite them to bring in product packaging and coupons, or newspaper ads from home that contain these words.

If You Can Read This. . .

Activity Format

Small group

Objective

Students will read common words recognized in environmental-print words.

Materials

- "If You Can Read This Chart" (page 165)
- a supply of environmental-print words
- chart paper
- marker
- glue
- pencils
- scissors

Preparation

1. Locate environmental-print words that contain common words familiar to the children.
2. Prepare four environmental-print words for each student.
3. Duplicate a copy of the "If You Can Read This Chart" for each student.

Procedure

1. Gather a small group of students at a table.
2. Remind students that they are able to read many words in the world around them. Ask them to name some of the words they can read on signs.
3. Tell them that reading environmental-print words is very much like reading regular printed words. If they can read A*pple* J*acks*, they can read the written word *apple*.
4. Show the students a word, such as P*izza* H*ut*. Ask the students to say the words. Then, ask the students to point out the word *pizza*. Draw attention to the style and color of the letters.
5. Next, write the word *pizza* on chart paper. Encourage the students to compare the written word to the word in the environmental print. What do they notice? How are they different? How are they similar?
6. Tell students that if they can read P*izza* H*ut*, they can read the written word *pizza*.
7. Distribute the "If You Can Read This Chart" to each student and provide each student with four environmental-print words.
8. Instruct each student to glue an environmental-print word in each box. Have the student identify the common word and then write the word at the bottom of the box.

If You Can Read This. . . . (cont.)

Sample Dialog

Teacher: (Teacher holds up *Pizza Hut*.) What does this say?

Student: *Pizza Hut!*

Teacher: Which of the two words is the word *pizza*?

Student: The first word. The word that begins with **P**.

Teacher: Great! If you can read *Pizza Hut*, you can read the word *pizza* when it is written in pencil or when it appears in a book. (Write the word *pizza* on chart paper.) Let's look at the word *pizza* in the sample and the one I wrote on the paper. How are they different?

Student: The one on the paper is written in marker. The word begins with an uppercase letter.

Teacher: How are they alike?

Student: The letters are shaped the same.

Assessment

Review the students' writing of the words and pay attention to their participation in the group activity.

Differentiation

- Challenge the students to use the words from the chart to write sentences.
- Encourage the students to locate other environmental print containing words they know. Invite them to bring in product packaging and coupons, or newspaper ads from home that contain these words.

If You Can Read This . . . Chart

Can You Read It Now?

Activity Format

Small group

Objective

Students will match environmental print with their written or typed (decontextualized) form.

Materials

- Flip Book templates on pages 168 and 169 (one set of templates for each child in the group)
- cardstock
- scissors
- marker
- hole puncher
- four small metal rings (or yarn)
- glue
- eight different environmental-print words
- marker
- chart paper

Preparation

1. To make a flip book, copy and cut out the front and back covers from cardstock.
2. Write a title on the cover of the book.
3. Cut out the flip book pages and cut each on the bold line.
4. Punch a hole in each circle on the covers and pages. Then, assemble the book by using the metal rings (or yarn). There should be eight half-pages on the top and eight on the bottom (between the covers).
5. Glue a different environmental-print word on each of the top pages. Write one of the environmental-print words on the bottom pages using a marker. The written words should be in random order.

Procedure

1. Gather a small group of students at a table.
2. Remind the students of previous lessons in which they were able to read the environmental-print word and then identify the same word in written form.
3. Ask them to name some of the words they can read. For example, if they can read *Play-Doh*, they read the word *play*. If they can read *Jack in the Box*, they can read the word *box*.
4. Show the students an environmental-print word and then write the word(s) on chart paper. Ask the students to compare the environmental print to the words on the chart paper. What do they notice?
5. Distribute a flip book to each student. Explain that the goal is to match an environmental-print word to the word in written form. To do this, a student flips through the pages to find the matching words.
6. When students find two matching pages, have them show you their matches.

Can You Read It Now? (cont.)

Sample Dialog

Teacher:	(Teacher holds up the word *Play-Doh*.) What does this say?
Student:	*Play-Doh!*
Teacher:	(Write the word *Play-Doh* on chart paper.) Can you read this word?
Student:	Yes, it's *Play-Doh*.
Teacher:	Great! How do you know that the words on the environmental print are the same words on the chart?
Student:	They both begin with **p**. They both end in **h**. They don't look exactly the same, but the letter shapes are alike.
Teacher:	Use your flip book to match environmental-print words to written words. When you find a match, hold up your book to show me.

Assessment

Review the students' environmental-print/written-word matches. Pay close attention to each student's ability to recognize the words in different forms.

Differentiation

- Challenge the students to use the words from their flip books in sentences.
- To increase the difficulty, construct each flip book with different environmental-print words. After a student matches the environmental print and words in one book, he or she can trade books with another student and continue the challenge.

Front and Back Covers

ABC
123

Flip Book Pages

Conclusion

It should be clear that environmental print has been overlooked in intentional instruction and as curriculum materials that build awareness of print, concepts of print, and the conventions of written language. It has been a connection between emergent reading and alphabetic decoding that until recently has gone unnoticed. There are many lessons embedded in print in the real world. As teachers, we can actively and creatively use these lessons in our classrooms to help children connect sounds to letters to the print around them.

An environmental-print curriculum can enrich your reading program and need not be complicated or time-consuming. Materials for this supplemental curriculum are as near as the pantry, newspaper, or grocery store. Assessment of how and when children use the environmental-print curriculum informs and guides your teaching. What each child knows about print and needs to learn will becomes clear as you progress through the lessons.

As you implement a curriculum of environmental print, keep in mind the following:

- Be very aware of the things that are capturing the attention of your students and are relevant in children's worlds. These are the things that will motivate them to read. Create your own games and activities that use familiar print to draw attention to different decoding skills.
- Consider using play centers stocked with props that are familiar and functional. In this setting, rather than using environmental print cutouts, the actual items are used. Literacy props using environmental print encourage natural play. Items you may consider include empty cereal boxes, fast-food menus, product packaging, signs, etc.
- Even the child with the most limited literacy experience may indeed hold a great deal of functional knowledge about print. Assess children's awareness of print in their environment so you have a clearer understanding of each child and what he or she needs next from your instruction.

Children and teachers alike respond enthusiastically to instructional lessons using environmental print. This is no surprise, as a real part of their world is acknowledged at school. Items that typically have home/life significance are valued and used as a basis for school instruction. Children and teachers participate in enjoyable, motivating, and meaningful activities that positively impact print awareness and a variety of decoding skills. There is an enormous world of potential resources just waiting for you to use in your literacy instruction.

Appendix A

Works Cited

Anderson G., and A. Markle. 1985. Cheerios, McDonald's, and Snickers: Bringing EP into the classroom. *Reading Education in Texas*: 30–35.

Berry, R. 2001. Children's environmental print: Reliability, validity, and relationship to early reading. Doctoral dissertation, University of North Carolina at Chapel Hill.

Christie, J. F., B.J. Enz, M. Gerard, and J. Prior. 2002. Using environmental print as teaching materials and Assessment tools. Paper presented at the International Reading Association annual convention, San Francisco, CA.

———. 2003a. Understanding how environmental print supports early literacy. Symposium presented at the Arizona State University Language and Literacy Conference, Tempe, AZ.

———. 2003b. Understanding how environmental print supports early literacy. Paper presented at the National Reading Conference, Scottsdale, AZ.

Christie, J. F., B. J. Enz, and C. Vukelich. 2002. *Teaching language and literacy, preschool through the elementary grades*. New York: Longman.

Cloer, T., J. Aldridge, and R. Dean. 1981/1982. Examining different levels of print awareness. *Journal of Language Experience* 4 (1/2): 25–33.

Duke, N. K., and V. Purcell-Gates. 2003, Genres at home and at school: Bridging the known to the new. *The Reading Teacher* 57 (1): 30–37.

Ferreiro, E., and A. Teberosky. 1982. Literacy before schooling. Exeter, NH: Heinemann.

Goodman, Y. 1986. Children coming to know literacy. In *Emergent literacy: Writing and reading*, ed. W. H. Teale and E. Sulzby, 1–14. Norwood, NJ: Ablex.

Harste, J., C. Burke, and V. Woodward. 1982. Children's language and world: Initial encounters with print. In *Reader meets author/bridging the gap: A psycholinguistic and sociolinguistic perspective*, ed. J. A. Langer and M. T. Smith-Burke, 105–131. Newark, DE: International Reading Association.

Masonheimer, P., P. Drum, and L. Ehri. 1984. Does environmental print identification lead children into word reading? *Journal of Reading Behavior* 1:257–71.

NAEYC. 2001. What does it look like and what does it take?: Supporting early literacy. White House Summit on Early Childhood Cognitive Development, Washington, D.C.

National Institute of Child Health and Human Development. 2000. *Teaching children to read: An evidence-based Assessment of the scientific research literature on reading and its implications for reading instruction*. Report of the National Reading Panel. Washington, DC: U.S. Government Print Office.

Orellana, M. F., and A. Hernandez. 2003. Talking the walk: Children reading urban environmental print. In *Promising Practices for Urban Reading Instruction*, ed. P.A. Mason and J.S. Schumm, 33.

Prior, J., and M. R. Gerard. 2004. *Environmental print in the classroom: Meaningful connections for learning to read*. Newark, DE: International Reading Association.

Simmons, D., B. Gunn, S. Smith, and E. J. Kameenui. 1994. Phonological awareness: Application of instructional design. LD Forum 19 (2): 7–10.

U.S. Department of Education. 2000. No Child Left Behind. **http://www.ed.gov/nclb/landing.jhtml**

U.S. Department of Education. 2001. Early Reading First. **http://www.ed.gov/programs/earlyreading/index.html**

Xu, S. H., and A. L. Rutledge. 2003. Chicken starts with ch! Kindergartners learn through environmental print. *Young Children* 58 (2): 44–51.

English-Language Learner Support

In our diverse society, classrooms are filled more and more with children who do not speak English as their first language. This presents a challenge for many teachers. The following are tips and ideas that will assist you in adapting lessons in this book for use with English-language learners.

Strategies for English-Language Learners

Use these general strategies to begin creating a classroom that is friendly and inviting to second-language learners.

- Work with ELL teachers and staff.
- Develop a library in your classroom with a wide range of books.
- Expand the curriculum with activities that draw on the cultural backgrounds of students.
- Encourage the contributions of students and their families.
- Establish classroom routines that incorporate learning.

Strategies for Planning

As you plan instruction, use these strategies to enhance the learning of second-language learners.

- Speak slowly and clearly so students have time to process the new language.
- Embed skills in a meaningful context.
- Access students' background to build understanding.
- Use repetition as a key to effective learning.
- Design curriculum that accommodates various learning styles and intelligences.
- Create a language-rich environment with lots of talk and print.
- Provide hands-on learning experiences.
- Model learning in a direct, systematic way.
- Present information in small manageable chunks.
- Limit new vocabulary to five new words per lesson.
- Adapt lessons for small group instruction.

English–Language Learner Support (cont.)

Teaching Strategies

To make your teaching style more effective with second-language learners, include these teaching strategies to enhance instruction.

- Pair novice English speakers with more skilled peers.
- Use graphic and advanced organizers to visually display information.
- Use visuals that are familiar to the students.
- Actively teach using body language, signals, and dramatizations to illustrate concepts.
- Allow students to express comprehension through drawing.
- Encourage students to equate concepts, words, and environmental print to home experiences.

Evaluation and Assessment

For continual assessment of ELL student progress, use these formal and informal strategies:

- Include students in the assessment process.
- Use authentic learning experiences.
- Repeat directions to ensure clarity.
- Allow ample time.
- Evaluate progress over time.

Extension Ideas for Centers

Our classrooms are filled with diverse learners who will finish at differing rates, require more assistance, and absorb new information and concepts in different ways.

In a learning center:

- Place the environmental-print words with specific categories for the students to sort.
- Encourage students to continue skill development.
- Encourage students to repeat the activity independently.
- Have students create environmental print-patterns by color, word size, or rhyming.
- Use alternative ways to write environmental-print words (writing in chalk, sand, hair gel, and shaving cream; using slate boards, sand paper, gel pens on black paper; or individual whiteboards).
- Post category labels on the wall or simply set them on a table. Encourage children to sort environmental-print words independently or in small groups.
- Instruct students to create songs that reflect learning.
- Have students record their own voices as they read and reread environmental-print words.
- Encourage struggling learners to say and record beginning letter sounds in environmental print.
- Have students sort environmental print by beginning, ending, or middle letters of the words.
- Have students work together to decode new environmental-print words.
- Provide letter tiles or magnetic letters for spelling environmental-print words.
- Provide students with typed environmental-print words to sound out and read.
- Have students practice identifying consonants and vowels in environmental print and in other words.
- Provide rebus messages for students to read.
- Ask students to write rebus messages to friends or family.

Extension Ideas for Fast Finishers

Increase the difficulty level of any lesson by:

- Having students repeat the activity with more difficult words.
- Using new vocabulary words, student names, and sight words.
- Reading and rereading words featured in the lessons.
- Having students direct the lesson contents in small groups or pairs.
- Instructing students to locate words in books, magazines, and newspapers.
- Having students use decontextualized words from environmental print in their writing.
- Having students write complete sentences using the common words they find.
- Having students write lists of words (real or nonsense) that rhyme with environmental-print words.
- Having students identify syllables in long environmental-print words.
- Including more than one environmental-print word beginning with the same letter, providing students the opportunity to recognize the same letter printed in different forms.
- Using environmental-print words at differing levels of decontextualization.

Extension Ideas for Family Involvement

To involve families in early reading development:

- Send the words home with the student to sort with family members.
- Challenge students to add new words to the group with family members.
- Have students take environmental-print words home to read with family members.
- Encourage students to locate environmental-print words that contain common words.
- Invite students to bring product packaging, coupons, or newspaper ads to school.
- Encourage students and families to glue environmental-print words with selected beginning letters to construction paper.
- Encourage families to locate and cut out familiar words from magazines or newspapers.
- Instruct students to bring in environmental print from home that has different long and short vowel sounds.
- Have students and family members search through advertising to find a letter, the letter **s** for example, for creating an alphabet book.
- Check out completed environmental-print word books to students for home reading.
- Have students and family members create rebus messages using environmental print.
- Instruct students and family members to write complete stories together using environmental print rebus words.
- Have students echo-read their class-made books with family members.
- Instruct students to conduct surveys about family preferences related to environmental print items.